THE HISTORY AND LIVES OF THE MOST

NOTORIOUS PIRATES

AND THEIR CREWS

T0058382

THE HISTORY AND LIVES OF THE MOST NOTORIOUS PIRATES

AND THEIR CREWS

Captain Charles Johnson

Foreword by C. Lovat Fraser

Skyhorse Publishing

Skyhorse Publishing books may be purchased in bulk at special discounts for sales promotion, corporate gifts, fund-raising, or educational purposes. Special editions can also be created to specifications. For details, contact the Special Sales Department, Skyhorse Publishing, 307 West 36th Street, 11th Floor, New York, NY 10018 or info@skyhorsepublishing.com.

Skyhorse® and Skyhorse Publishing® are registered trademarks of Skyhorse Publishing, Inc.®, a Delaware corporation.

Visit our website at www.skyhorsepublishing.com.

10 9 8 7 6 5 4 3 2 1

Library of Congress Cataloging-in-Publication Data is available on file.

Cover design by Owen Corrigan

Print ISBN: 978-1-62914-539-6
Ebook ISBN: 978-1-62914-986-8

Printed in the United States of America

CONTENTS

LIST OF ILLUSTRATIONS

FOREWORD

Time, though a good Collector, is not always a reliable Historian. That is to say, that although nothing of interest or importance is lost, yet an affair may be occasionally invested with a glamour that is not wholly its own. I venture to think that Piracy has fortuned in this particular. We are apt to base our ideas of Piracy on the somewhat vague ambitions of our childhood; and I suppose, were such a thing possible, the consensus of opinion in our nurseries as to a future profession in life would place Piracy but little below the glittering heights of the police force and engine-driving. Incapable of forgetting this in more mature years, are we not inclined to deck Her (the "H" capital, for I speak of an ideal), if not in purple and fine linen, at least with a lavish display of tinsel and gilt? Nursery lore remains with us, whether we would or not, for all our lives; and generations of ourselves, as schoolboys and pre-schoolboys, have tricked out Piracy in so resplendent a dress that she has fairly ousted in our affections, not only her sister profession of "High Toby and the Road," but every other splendid and villainous vocation. Yet Teach, Kid, and Avery were as terrible or grim as Duval, Turpin, and Sheppard were courtly or whimsical. And the terrible is a more vital affair than the whimsical. Is it, then, unnatural that, after a lapse of nigh on two centuries, we should shake our wise heads and allow that which is still nursery within us to deplore the loss of those days when we ran before a favouring "Trade" the very good chance of being robbed, maimed, or murdered by Captain Howel Davis or Captain Neil Gow? It is as well to remember that the "Captains" in this book were seamen whose sole qualifications to the title were ready wit, a clear head, and, maybe, that certain indefinable "power of the eye" that is the birth-right of all true leaders. The piratical hero of our childhood is traceable in a great extent to the "thrillers," toy plays, and penny theatres of our grandfathers. Here our Pirate was, as often as not, a noble, dignified, if gloomy gentleman, with a leaning to Byronic soliloquy. Though stern in exterior, his heart could (and would) melt at the distresses of the heroine. Elvira's eyes were certain to awaken in his mind the recollection of "other eyes as innocent as thine, child." In short, he was that most touching of all beings, the

Hero-cum-Villain. And it was with a sigh of relief that we saw him at the eleventh hour, having successfully twitted the "Government Men" and the Excise (should he have an additional penchant for smuggling), safely restored to the arms of the long-suffering possessor of the other eyes.

Alas! this little book mentions no Poll of Portsmouth, nor does it favour us with a "Yeo, heave, oh!" nor is there so very much "cut and thrust" about it. It was written in that uninspiring day when Pirates were a very real nuisance to such law-abiding folk as you and I; but it has the merit of being written, if not by a Pirate, at least by one who came into actual contact with them. I am not at all sure that "merit" is the right word to use in this instance, for to be a Pirate does not necessarily ensure you making a good author. Indeed, it might almost be considered as a ban to the fine literary technique of an Addison or a Temple. It has, however, the virtue of being in close touch with some of the happenings chronicled. Not that our author saw above a tithe of what he records—had he done so he would have been "set a-sundrying" at Execution Dock long before he had had the opportunity of putting pen to paper; but, as far as posterity was concerned, he was lucky in his friend William Ingram—evidently a fellow of good memory and a ready tongue—"who," as our author states in his Preface, "was a Pirate under Anstis, Roberts, and many others," and who eventually was hanged in good piratical company on the 11th of June, 1714.

The actual history of the little book, the major part of which is here reprinted, is as follows:

Its full title is "The History and Lives of all the most Notorious Pirates and their Crews," and the fifth edition, from which our text is taken, was printed in 1735. A reproduction of the original title-page is given on the following page.

As a matter of fact, the title is misleading. How could a book that makes no mention of Morgan or Lollonois be a history of all the most notorious Pirates? It deals with the last few years of the seventeenth century and the first quarter of the eighteenth, a period that might with justice be called "The Decline and Fall of Piracy," for after 1730 Piracy became but a mean broken-backed affair that bordered perilously on mere sea-pilfering.

A little research into the book's history shows us that it is consistent throughout, and that it is a "piracy," in the publisher's sense of the word, of a much larger and more pretentious work by Captain Charles Johnson, entitled, "A General History of the Pyrates from their first Rise and Settlement in the Island of Providence to the Present Time; With the Remarkable Actions and Adventures of the two Female Pyrates Mary Read and Anne Bonny."

This was published in London, in like this in original by Charles Rivington in 1724. A second edition, considerably augmented, was issued later in the same year, a third edition in the year following, and a fourth edition—in two volumes, as considerable additions in

THE

HISTORY *and* LIVES
Of all the most Notorious
PIRATES,
AND THEIR
CREWS;

From Capt. Avery, who first settled at *Madagascar*, to
Captain *John Gow*, and *James Williams*, his Lieutenant,
etc. who were hang'd at *Execution Dock, June 11.* 1725,
for Piracy and Murther; and afterwards hang'd in
Chains between *Blackwall* and *Deptford*. And in this
Edition continued down to the present Year 1735.

Giving a more full and true Account than any yet
Publish'd of all their Murthers, Piracies, Maroonings,
Places of Refuge, and Ways of Living.

THE FIFTH EDITION

Adorned with Twenty Beautiful CUTS, being the
Representation of each Pirate.

To which is prefixed,
An Abstract of the Laws against Piracy.

LONDON:

Printed for *A. Bettesworth* and *C. Hitch*, at the *Red Lyon*
in *Pater-noster-Row*; *R. Ware*, at the *Sun* and *Bible* in
Amen. Corner; and *J. Hodges* at the *Looking-glass* on
London-bridge, 1735.

the form of extra "Lives," and an appendix necessi-
tated a further volume—in 1725.

This two-volume edition contained the history of
the following Pirates: Avery, Martel, Teach, Bonnet,
England, Vane, Rackham, Davis, Roberts, Anstis,
Morley, Lowther, Low, Evans, Phillips, Spriggs, Smith,
Misson, Bowen, Kid, Tew, Halsey, White, Condent,
Bellamy, Fly, Howard, Lewis, Cornelius, Williams,
Burgess, and North, together with a short abstract on
the Statute and Civil Law in relation to "Pyracy," and
an appendix, completing the Lives in the first volume,
and correcting some mistakes.

The work evidently enjoyed a great vogue, for it
was translated into Dutch by Robert Hannebo, of
Amsterdam, in 1727, and issued there, with several
"new illustrations," in 12mo. A German version by
Joachim Meyer was printed at Gosslar in the following year, while in France it saw the light as an
appendix to an edition of Esquemeling's "Histoire des
Avanturiers," 1726.

But little is known of the author, Captain Charles
Johnson, excepting that he flourished from 1724 to
1736, and it is more than probable that the name by
which we know him is an assumed one. It is possible
that his knowledge of Pirates and Piracy was of such a
nature to have justified awkward investigations on the
part of His Majesty's Government.

There is one thing that we do know for certain
about him, and that is that the worthy Captain's spelling, according to the pirated version of his book, was

indefinite even for his own day. He was one of those inspired folk who would be quite capable of spelling "schooner" with three variations in as many lines. In this edition the spelling has been more or less modernized.

Lastly, it is to be remembered that the ships of this period, according to our modern ideas, would be the veriest cockle-shells, and so that we should know what manner of vessel he refers to in these pages, I had recourse to a friend of mine whose knowledge of things nautical is extensive enough to have gained for him the coveted "Extra Master's Certificate," and who was kind enough to supply me with the following definitions:

SLOOP.

A vessel rigged as a cutter, but with one head-sail only set on a very short bowsprit.

SCHOONER.   TOPSAIL SCHOONER.

Two-masted vessels, fore and aft rigged, sometimes having square topsails on the fore-mast.

BRIGANTINE.

A two-masted vessel, square rigged on fore-mast.

GALLEY.

A large vessel rowed by oars and sometimes having auxiliary sail of various rigs.

PINK.

Probably a small, fast vessel used as a tender and despatch boat for river work.

SNOW.

A two-masted vessel with a stay, known as a "Horse," from the main-mast to the poop on which the trysail was set. Sometimes a spar was fitted instead of a stay. The rig was most likely of a brig (*i.e.*, a two-masted ship, square sails on both masts), and the triangular trysail set on the stay in bad weather or when hove to.

C. L. F.

THE LIFE OF
CAPTAIN AVERY

CAPTAIN JOHN AVERY

THE LIFE OF
CAPTAIN AVERY

HE was the son of John Avery, a victualler near *Plymouth*, in *Devonshire*, who in a few years was grown as opulent in his purse as in his body, by scoring two for one; and when he had so done, drinking the most of the liquor himself. By which means, and having a handsome wife, who knew her business as well as if she had been brought up to it from a child (which, indeed, she mostly was, her mother keeping the House before she married Mr. Avery), they soon became very rich and very able to give credit to a whole ship's crew upon their tickets, which in those days were sold for less than half their value.

Having but one child (afterwards the Captain), they at first resolved to bring him up a scholar, that he might advance the dignity of the family. But instead of learning his book, he was taught by such companions that he could soon swear to every point of his compass, which was a very diverting scene for the Boatswain and his crew, who were then drinking in the kitchen, having just received ten pounds apiece short allowance money on board the *Revenge*, every farthing of which they spent before leaving the house.

But as soon as their money was spent, they were all like to have been imprisoned by their Landlady for a riot, as she called it, so they were soon glad to sheer off, and he thought himself happiest that could get first aboard. Indeed, it would have been happy for them if they had, for the ship was unmoored and gone to sea; which put the Boatswain and his crew swearing in earnest, and not knowing what to do, they resolved to return to their Landlady, Mrs. Avery, at "the Sign of the *Defiance*." But she shut them out of doors, calling them a parcel of beggarly rascals, and swearing that if they would not go from the door she would send for the Constable; and notwithstanding all the entreaties and tears of her only son, who was then about six years of age, she could not be prevailed upon to let them in, so they were obliged to stroll about the street all night. In the morning, spying the ship at anchor, being driven back by contrary winds, they resolved to make the best of their way aboard; but on the way, whom should they meet but young Avery, who had no sooner seen them, but he cried after them. "Zounds," says the Boatswain, "let's take the young dog aboard, and his mother shall soon be glad to adjust the reckoning more to our satisfaction before she shall have her son."

This was agreed upon by all hands, and the boy was as willing as any of them. So, stepping into the boat, in about an hour's time they reached the ship, which they had no sooner boarded but they were brought before the Captain, who, being in want of hands, contented himself with bidding them all go to their business; for the wind turned about, and there was occasion for all hands to be at work to carry out the ship.

All this while young Avery was at the heels of the Boatswain, and was observed to swear two oaths to one of the Boatswain's; which being soon observed by the Captain, he inquired who brought that young rascal aboard.

To which the Boatswain replied that he did, that the boy's mother was his Landlady on shore, and he had taken him up in jest, but was afraid that they would now have to keep him in earnest.

When the hurry was a little over, the Captain commanded the boy to be brought to him in his cabin. He had not talked long to him before he took a fancy to him, telling him that if he would be a good boy, he should live with him.

He, being a mighty lover of children, would often divert himself by talking to the boy, till at length he took such a fancy to him, that he ordered him a little hammock in his own cabin, and none were so great as the Captain and his boy Avery, which had like to have proved very fatal to him; for Avery one night, observing the Captain to be very drunk with some passengers that were on board, got a lighted match and had like to have blown up the ship, had not the Gunner happened accidentally to follow him into the store-room. This made the Captain ever after very shy of his new Acquaintance, and Avery, after he had been well whipped, was ordered down into the hold, where he remained until they arrived at *Carolina*, which happened four or five days after.

The boy was given to a merchant, who, taking a fancy to him, put him to school; but he made so little progress in learning, and committed so many unlucky tricks, that the merchant, in about three years, shipped him off to his friends at *Plymouth* on board the *Nonesuch*, where he was no sooner arrived but his mother was overjoyed with the sight of her son, his father being dead about a month before his arrival.

And, indeed, it was thought the loss of their son broke his heart, for it was observed the father never held up his head after, the neighbours often reflecting upon him for his ill-usage of the seamen, who had spent so much money at his house; saying he could never expect that all his ill-gotten riches could prosper him, which so happened, as you shall hear presently. For his mother, dying soon after, the boy was left under the guardianship of one Mr. Lightfoot, a merchant, who, having great losses at sea, became a bankrupt, and so young Avery was left to look out after himself; there he continued for many years in pilfering and stealing till the country was too hot for him, when he betook him to sea again, where in time he became as famous for robbing as Cromwell for rebellion.

He entered himself on board the *Duke*, Captain Gibson Commander, being one of the two ships of twenty-four guns and one hundred men which were fitted out by the merchants of *Bristol* for the service of *Spain*, which they had no sooner done, but they were ordered by their agents at Bristol to sail for the *Groyne* to receive their orders.

On board one of which ships Avery, being at this time above twenty years old, entered himself, where he had not been long before he observed the Captain was much addicted to drunkenness.

He endeavoured to spirit up not only his own ship's crew, but having also given the word to part of the other ship's crew, the conspirators gave the signal.

At which the *Duchess*, as the other ship was named, put off her longboat; which the conspirators hailing were answered by the men in the boat, "Is your drunken Boatswain on board?" This being the word agreed upon, Avery answered, "All is safe;" upon which twenty lusty fellows came aboard and joined them, which they had no sooner done but they secured the hatches and went to work, putting to sea without any disorder, although there were several ships in the bay, amongst whom was a frigate of forty-four guns.

The Captain, by this time being awaked by the noise of the conspirators working the ship, rung the bell, inquiring what was the matter, to whom Avery and some of the crew replied, "Nothing. Are you mutinous in your cups? Can't you lie down, sleep, and be quiet?"

"No," saith the Captain. "I am sure something's the matter with the ship. Does she drive? What weather is it? Is it a storm?"

Saith Avery: "Cannot you lie quiet while you are quiet? I tell you all's well; we are at sea in a fair wind and good weather."

"At sea," saith the Captain; "that can't be."

"Be not frightened," saith Avery, "and I'll tell you. You must note, I am now the Captain of the ship; nay, you must turn out, for this is my cabin, and I am bound for *Madagascar*, to make my own fortune as well as my companions."

The Captain, being more terrified than ever, did not know what to say, which Avery perceiving, bid him take heart. "For," saith he, "if you will join me and these brave fellows, my companions, in time you may get some post under me. If not, step into the longboat and get about your business."

This the Captain was glad to hear, but yet began to expostulate with them upon the injustice of such doings. Saith Avery: "What do I care? Every man for himself. Come, come, Captain, if you will go, get you gone; the longboat waits for you, and if there be any more cowards in the ship, you may all go together." Which words so affrighted the whole crew, that there was not above nine or ten of them that durst venture, who made the best of their way to the shore as fast as they could, and thought they were well off.

The Captain was no sooner gone, but they called a Council, which agreed to own Avery as their Captain; which he accepted with all humility imaginable, seeming to excuse himself on account of his inexperience at sea. But he did it so artfully that it more confirmed them in the good opinion of their choice. "Gentlemen," said he, "what we have done we must live or die by; let us all be hearty and of one mind, and I don't question but we shall make our fortune in a little time. I propose that we sail first to Madagascar, where we may settle a correspondence, in order to secure our retreats, whenever we think fit to lie by."

To which they all agreed, "Nemine contradicente."

"But hold," saith Avery; "it is necessary that we make some order among us, for the better governing of the ship's crew." Which were in a few days drawn up by the clerk of the ship.

And Avery promising them vast things, they all came into them at last, although some things went very much against the grain of many of them. It took up all their spare time till they arrived at *Madagascar*, where they saw a Ship lying at the N.E. part of the Island, with which the men had run away from *New England*; and seeing Avery, they supposed that he had been sent after them to take them, but Avery soon undeceived them, and promised them protection; therefore they resolved to sail together. In the whole company, there was not above ten that pretended to any skill in navigation; for Avery himself could neither write nor read very well, he being chosen Captain of the *Duke* purely for his courage and contrivance.

In the latitude of *Descada*, one of the Islands, they took two other sloops, which supplied them with provisions, and then they agreed to proceed to the West Indies; and coming to *Barbadoes*, they fell in with a ship for *London* with twelve guns, from which they took some clothes and money, ten barrels of powder, ten casks of beef, and several other goods, and five of her men, and then let her go. From thence he went to the Island of *Dominica*, and watered; there he met with six *Englishmen*, who willingly entered with Avery. They stayed not long before they sailed for the *Granada* Island to clean their ships; which being known to the *French* Colony, the Governor of *Martenico* sent four sloops well manned after them. But they stayed there not long, but made the best of their way for *Newfoundland*, entering the harbour of Trepasse with black colours, drums beating, and trumpets sounding.

It is impossible to relate the havoc they made there, burning all before them. When they left *Newfoundland* they sailed for the *West Indies*, and from thence to the Island *Descada*, it being judged the most convenient place, at that time of the year, to meet with a rich booty.

From hence they steered towards the *Arabian* Coast, near the River *Indus*, where, spying a sail, they gave chase. At their near approach she hoisted *Mogul* colours and seemed as if she would stand upon her defence, whilst Avery contented himself by cannonading her at a distance, which made many of his men begin to mutiny, thinking him a coward.

But Avery knew better, and commanding his sloops to attack her, one in the Bow, and the rest on the Quarter, clapt her on board, upon which she struck her colours and yielded. Aboard her was one of the Mogul's own daughters, with several persons of distinction, who were carrying rich offerings of jewels and other valuable presents to *Mecca;* which booty was the more considerable, because these people always travel with great magnificence, having all their slaves and attendants always with them, besides jewels and great sums of money to defray the charges. But Avery, not content with this, seized the young Princess, and taking her with him into his own ship, made the best of his way to *Madagascar*, where she soon broke her heart and died. Also her father, the Great Mogul, did no sooner hear of it but he threatened all *Europe* with revenge. And when he knew they were *Englishmen* who had captured his daughter and robbed him, he threatened to send a mighty army, with fire and sword, to extirpate all the *English* from their settlements on the *Indian* Coasts, which gave no small uneasiness to the *Indian Company* at *London*, when they heard of it.

CAPTAIN JOHN RACKHAM, AND HIS CREW

CAPTAIN JOHN RACKHAM

CAPTAIN JOHN RACKHAM, AND HIS CREW

JOHN RACKHAM was Quarter-Master to *Vane's* Company, till *Vane* was turned out for not fighting the French Man-of-War, and Rackham put in Captain in his place, which happened about the 24th day of November, 1718. His first cruise was among the *Caribbe* Islands, where he took and plundered several vessels. Afterwards, to the windward of *Jamaica*, he fell in with a *Madeira* Man, which he detained till he had made his market out of her, and then restored her to her Master, suffering Hosea Tisdel, a tavern-keeper at Jamaica, whom he had taken among his Prizes, to go aboard her, she being bound for that Island.

Afterwards he sailed towards the Island *Bermuda*, where he took a Ship bound to *England* from *Carolina*, and a small Ship from *New England*, both which he carried to the *Bahama Islands*, and there clean'd. But staying too long in that neighbourhood, Captain

Rogers sent out a Sloop well mann'd, which retook both the Prizes, the Pirate making his escape.

From hence they proceeded to the back of *Cuba*, where Rackham staid a long time with his Delilahs, till their Provision was consumed, when he concluded it time to look out for more. As he was putting to Sea, a *Garda del Costa* came in with a small *English* Sloop, which he had taken as an interloper on that coast. The *Spaniards* seeing the Pirate, attacked her; but finding he could not come to her that night, because she lay close behind a little island, he warps into the channel, to make sure of her in the morning. Upon this Rackham took his Crew into the Boat, with their pistols and cutlasses, and falls aboard the *Spaniards* in the night, without being discovered, telling them, if they spoke a word they were dead men: And so shipping their cables, drove out to sea, commanding them to take the Boat, and go aboard their Sloop immediately, or else they were all dead men. Afterwards they waking the Captain and his men in the Hammocks, who rose full of their expectation of the Prizes, they sent them aboard their empty Sloop.

In the beginning of September, they went off of the French part of *Hispaniola*, where they took two or three *Frenchmen* on board, that were looking after some cattle grazing near the waterside. Then plundered two Sloops, they returned to *Jamaica*, where they took a Schooner.

Rackham continuing about this Island longer than a Man of his business ought to have done, gave time to a

Canoe, which he had surprised in *Ocho* Bay, to inform the Governor of *Jamaica* of his civilities to all he met with going or coming from the Island. Thereupon a Sloop was sent out in quest of him, well mann'd and arm'd, under Captain Barnet, to repay him for all his good-natured actions, and, if possible, to bring him into the Island. In the mean time Rackham met, near the *Negril* Point, a small Pettiauger, which, upon sight of him, ran ashore, and landed her men; but Rackham hailing them, desired the Pettiauger's men to come aboard him, and drink a bowel of punch; swearing, *They were all Friends and would do no Harm.* Hereupon they agreed to his request, and went aboard him, though it proved fatal to every one of them, they being nine in all. For, they were no sooner got aboard, and had laid down their muskets and cutlasses, in order to take up their pipes, and make themselves merry with their new acquaintance over a can of Flip, but Captain Barnet's Sloop was in sight, which soon put a damp to all their merriment: Finding she stood directly towards them, they immediately weighed their anchor and stood off. Barnet gave them chase, and having the advantage of the wind, soon came up with her, gave her a broadside or two, and, after a very small dispute, took her and his nine new guests, and brought them all together into *Port-Royal* in *Jamaica*, in about a fortnight's time.

November the 10th, 1720, a Court of Admiralty was held at *St. Jago de la Vega,* where the following Persons were tried and convicted of Piracy, and accordingly Sentence of Death was passed upon them by the Governor, viz.: *John Rackham*, Captain; *George Fetherstone*, Master; *Richard Corner*, Quarter-Master; *John Davis, John Howel, Patrick Carty, Thomas Earle, James Dobbin*, and *Noah Harwood*; five of whom was hang'd the next day at *Gallows-point*, and the rest the day after. The three first were taken and hanged in chains; *Rackham* at *Plumb-point, Fetherstone* at *Bush-key*, and *Corner* at *Gun-key*.

But what was yet more strange was the conviction of the nine guests, that knew nothing of the matter, or at least they pretended so; but the People would not believe them, because it was proved that they came on board with pistols and cutlasses: However, they were so much favoured as to have the Court adjourned to the 24th of January following, to give a better account of themselves than at the time appeared to the Court: Beside, the Jury also then wanted sufficient evidence to prove the piratical intention of going aboard the said Sloops. The two *Frenchmen* taken by Rackham from the Island of *Hispaniola*, deposed, That *John Eaton, Edward Warner, Thomas Baker, Thomas Quick, John Cole, Benjamin Palmer, Walter Rouse, John Hanson*, and *John Howard*, came on board the Pirate's Sloop at *Negril Point* in *Jamaica*. Indeed they owned, That at first sight of them, they run away from Rackham's Sloop, but that he hailing them, they returned, and Rackham sent his canoe ashore to fetch them aboard him, when they saw them all armed with guns and cutlasses, which they brought with them; and that when they were chased by Captain Barnet, they were frank and free, some drinking and walking about the deck not at all dispirited; during which time there was a great gun, and small arms, fired by the Pirate Sloop at Captain Barnet's Sloop; but that they could not say that the Prisoners were any way concerned in it: However, they were certain that when Captain Barnet's Sloop fired at Rackham's, the Prisoners at the Bar went under Deck, for cowardice, as they supposed; not so much as once peeping up during the time of the whole action: But when Captain Barnet drew nigh to them to board them, all of them came up, and helped to row the sloop, in order to escape from him: And that Rackham's men and they seemed to agree very well together, and that they did verily believe they were all of a Party, having heard them say, when they came on board, *They liked them never the worse for being Pirates, since they were all honest Boys, and loved their Bottles.*

To which the Prisoners answered, in their own defense; that they were a great way off from friends and acquaintance, and, therefore it was impossible to have any one to give an account of them. That they were very honest pains-taking men, and came out to go a-turtling to provide for their families; accordingly going ashore at *Negril* Point they saw a Sloop, with a white pendant, making towards them, whereupon they took up their arms, which were no other but what all people carry upon such occasions, and ran into the woods, to hide themselves among the bushes, not knowing what she might be. But when they hailed them and told them they were *Englishmen*, they ventured out, and came aboard them, as they desired, to drink a bowl of punch, they being poor men, who get their livelihood very hardily, and such a thing was very acceptable to them. But when they came on board the Sloop, to their very great surprise, they found they were Pirates; upon which they begged to be released; but Rackham swore, that if they did not stay and assist them against that Sloop that was coming down against them, he would cut all their throats. So being compelled thereunto by Rackham and his men, to save their Lives, they did assist him, and with no other design but to prevent their being cut in pieces, but as soon as Captain Barnet came up with them, they all very readily and willingly submitted.

This being all they had to say in their own defense, the Prisoners were ordered from the Bar: The Court were divided in their Judgments; but the majority were of opinion, that they were all guilty of the Piracy and Felony they were charged with; thereupon they all received Sentence of Death, as usual in such cases, the Judge making a very pathetic Speech to them, exhorting them to bear their sufferings patiently, assuring them, that if they were innocent, which he very much doubted, then their reward would be greater in the Other World: But everybody must own their case was very hard in this.

February the 17th, *John Eaton, Thomas Quick*, and *Thomas Baker*, were accordingly executed at *Gallows-Point*; and the next day, *John Cole, John Howard*, and *Benjamin Palmer*, underwent the same fate at Kingston. The other three got a reprieve, they being against going aboard the Pirate's Sloop, and are now living.

CAPTAIN SPRIGGS, AND HIS CREW

CAPTAIN SPRIGGS,
AND HIS GREW

SPRIGGS sailed at first with Lowe, and came away with him from Lowther. Afterwards Lowe took a ship of twelve guns on the Coast of *Guinea*, called the *Delight*, which Spriggs went off on board with twenty men, and leaving Lowe in the night, came to the *West Indies*. In their passage they made a Black Ensign, which they called the *Jolly Roger*, with a skeleton in the middle holding a dart in one hand, striking a bleeding heart; and in the other an hour-glass; and being hoisted, they fired all their guns to salute Spriggs, whom they chose Captain, and then went to look out for prey.

In their voyage they took a *Portuguese* barque, wherein they had rich plunder. Near *St. Lucia*, they took a Sloop belonging to *Barbadoes*, which they first plundered, and then burnt, forcing some of the men into their service, and beating, in a barbarous manner, those that refused to join with them, and afterwards sent them away in the Boat, half dead with their wounds, the rest got to *Barbadoes*, with much ado, though some of them died soon after of their cuts and slashes. After this they took a *Martinico* Man, which they used in like manner, save that they did not burn the ship. Then running down to the Leeward, they took one Captain Hawkins coming from *Jamaica*, laden with Logwood; out of which, they took her stores, arms, and ammunition, and what they did not want they threw over-board; they cut the cables to pieces, knocked down the cabins, broke the windows, and did what mischief they could, taking Burridge and Stephens, the two Mates, and some other Hands, by force; and then after keeping her a week, they let her go. On the 27th they took a *Rhode* Island Sloop, compelling the Captain, and all his men, to go on board the Pirate: One of them not being willing to stay with them, they told him he should have a discharge presently, which was to receive ten lashes from every man on board.

The next day Burridge signed their Articles; which pleased them so much, that they fired all the Guns, and made him Master, spending that day in rejoicings and drinking healths.

The First of *April* they spied a sail, and gave her chase all night, believing she had been a *Spaniard*; but when they came up to her, and gave her a broadside, she cried out for Quarters, which made them cease firing, and ordered the Captain to come aboard, which proved to be Captain Hawkins, whom they had dismissed three days before, not worth a groat. Two days after, they anchored at *Ratran*, not far from *Honduras*, and put ashore Captain Hawkins, and several others, giving them powder and ball, and a musquet, and then left them to shift as well as they could. Here they staid three weeks, when two men came in a canoe, that had been left in another Maroon Island near *Benecca*, and carried them thither. A fortnight after they espied a Sloop at sea, which had lately escaped from the *Spaniards* at the Bay of *Honduras*, which, upon a signal stood in and took them all off.

At an Island to the westward, the Pirates cleaned their ship, and then sailed towards *St. Christophers* to meet Captain Moor.

Spriggs next stood towards *Bermudas*, where he took a Schooner belonging to *Boston*, from which he took all the men, and sunk the vessel.

Instead of going to *Newfoundland*, they came back to the Islands, and on the 8th of June, to windward of *St. Christophers*, they took a Sloop, Nicholas Trot, Master, belonging to *St. Eustatia*, whose men they hoisted as high as the main fore-tops, and so let them fall down again; then whipping them about the deck, they gave Trot his Sloop, and let him go, keeping only two of his men, besides the plunder. Two or three days after, they took a ship coming from *Rhode Island* to *St. Christophers*, laden with provisions and some horses, and burnt ship, men, and horses: Since when Spriggs has not been heard of: though it is supposed he went to *Madagascar*, to spend, in rioting and wantonness, his ill gotten plunder; till by a letter from *Jamaica*, of the 2nd of March last, we understood, that he had been again at the Bay of *Honduras*, and taken sixteen Sail.

CAPTAIN EDWARD LOWE, AND HIS CREW

CAPTAIN EDWARD LOWE

CAPTAIN EDWARD LOWE,
AND HIS CREW

EDWARD LOWE, born at *Westminster*, very early began the Trade of Plundering; for if any child refused him what he had, he must fight him. When he grew bigger, he took to Gaming among Blackshoe Boys upon the *Parade*, with whom he used to play the *Whole Game*, as they call it; that is, cheat every body, and if they refused, they had to fight him.

Ned went to Sea with his eldest Brother, and leaving him in *New-England*, he worked in a Rigging House, at Boston, for some time, when not liking that, he returned to *England* to see his Mother, with whom he did not stay long before he took his leave of her, for the last time, as he said, and returned to *Boston*, where he shipped himself in a Sloop that was bound to the Bay of *Honduras*; and when he arrived there, he was made Patron of the Boat, to bring the logwood on board to lade the ship; where he differing with the Captain about the hurry of taking the logwood on board, Lowe takes up a loaden Musquet, and fired at him; then putting off the Boat, he, with twelve of his companions, goes to sea. Next day they met a small vessel, which they took, made a Black Flag, and declared War against all the world. From hence they proceed to the Island of the *Grand Caimanes*, where they met with George Lowther, who took him under his protection as an ally, without any formal Treaty; which Lowe readily agreed to. But parting with Lowther on the 28th of May, as we have already given in an account in Lowther's Life, Lowe took a vessel belonging to *Amboy*, which he plundered, and then stood away to the South East, by which he avoided two Sloops which the Governor had sent to take him from *Rhode* Island.

July the 12th, he sailed into the Harbour of Port *Rosemary*, where he found 13 small vessels at anchor, whom he told they would have no quarters if they resisted; which so frightened the Masters of the vessels, that they all yielded. Out

of them he took whatever he wanted, keeping for his own use a Schooner of 80 Tons, on board of which he put 10 Carriage Guns, and 50 men, and named her the *Fancy* making himself captain, and appointing Charles Harris Captain of the Brigantine. Making up a complement of 80 men out of the vessels, some by force, and others by their own inclinations, he sailed away from *Mablehead*, and soon after he met two Sloops bound for *Boston*, with provisions for the garrison; but there being an officer and soldiers on board, he thought it the safest way, after some small resistance, to let them go on about their business.

They then steered for the *Leeward* Islands; but in their voyage met with such a hurricane, as had not been known in the memory of man. After the storm was over, they got safe to one of the small Islands of the *Carribees*, and there refitted their vessels as well as they could. As soon as the Brigantine was ready, they took a short cruise, leaving the Schooner in the harbour till their return; which had not been many days at sea, before she met a ship that had lost all her masts, on board of which they went, and took, in money and goods, to the value of 1000*l*. Upon this success, the Brigantine returned to the Schooner, which being then ready to sail, they agreed to go to the *Azores*, or Western Islands, where Lowe took a *French* Ship of 32 Guns, and in *St. Michael's* Road, he took several sail that were lying there, without firing a gun. Being in great want of water, he sent to the Governor of *St. Michael's* for a supply, promising upon that condition, to release the Ships he had taken, otherwise to burn them all; which the Governor, for the sake of the

Ships, agreed to. Thereupon he released six, keeping only the *Rose* Pink, of which he took the Command.

The Pirates took several of the Guns out of the ships, and mounted them on board the *Rose*. Lowe ordered the Schooner to lie in the Fare between *St. Michael's* and *St. Mary's*, where he met with Captain Carter in the *Wright* Galley; who, defending himself, they cut and mangled him and his men in a barbarous manner; after which, they were for burning the ship, but contented themselves with cutting her cable, rigging, and sails to pieces, and so left her to the mercy of the seas. From hence they sailed to the Island of *Maderas*, where they took a fishing boat, with two old men and a boy in her, one of whom they sent ashore, demanding a boat of water, otherwise they would kill the old man, which being complied with, the old man was discharged. From hence they sailed to the *Canaries*, and thence continued their course for the *Cape de Verde* Islands, where they took a ship called the *Liverpool Merchant*, from which they took 300 gallons of brandy, two guns and carriages, besides six of the men, and then obliged them to go to the Isle of *May*. They also took two *Portugueze* ships bound to Brazil, and three Sloops from *St. Thomas's* bound to *Curaso*: All of which they plundered, and let them go, except one Sloop, by which they heard that two Gallies were expected at the Western Islands. Her they manned, and sent in quest of these Ships whilst they careened the *Rose* at *Cape de Verde;* but the Sloop missing the prey, was reduced to great want of water and provisions, so that they ventured to go ashore *St. Michael's*, and pass for Traders; where, being suspected by the Governor, they were conducted into the Castle, and provided for as long as they lived.

Lowe's ship was overset a-careening, so that he was reduced to his old Schooner, aboard of which there went about an hundred as bold rogues as ever was hanged, and sailed to the *West-Indies*, where they took a rich *Portugueze* ship bound Home from *Bahia*, putting to the torture several of the men, who confest the Captain flung into the sea a bag of 11000 Moidores. This made Lowe swear a thousand oaths; and after cutting off his lips, he murdered him and all his Crew, being 36 men.

After this, they cruised to the Northward, and took several vessels and then steered for the Bay of *Honduras*, where they took five *English* Sloops, and a Pink, and a *Spaniard* of 6 Guns and 70 men, whom they killed every man; which being done they rummaged the *Spanish* Ship, bringing all the booty on board their own vessel.

In the next cruise, between the *Leeward Islands* and the Main, they took two Snows from Jamaica to Liverpool, and just after a Ship called the *Amsterdam Merchant*, the Captain thereof he slit his nose, cut his ears off, and then plundered the ship and let her go. Afterwards he took a Sloop bound to *Amboy*, of whose men he tied lighted matches between the fingers, which burnt the flesh off the bones, and afterwards set them ashore in an uninhabited part of the country, as also other ships which fell a prey to those villains.

One of His Majesty's Men-of-War called the *Greyhound*, of 20 guns and 120 men, hearing of their barbarous actions, went in search of them and, seeing the Pirates, allowed Lowe to chase them at first, till they were in readiness to engage him, and when he was within gunshot, tacked about and stood towards him. The Pirates edged away under the Man-of-War's stern, making a running fight for about two hours. But little wind happening, the Pirates gained from her; thereupon the *Greyhound* left off firing, and turned all her hands to her oars, and came up with them, when the fight was renewed with a brisk fire on both sides, till the *Ranger's* main-yard was shot down; upon which, the *Greyhound* pressing close, *Lowe* bore away and left his consort, who seeing the cowardice of his Commadore, and that there was no possibility of escaping, called out for quarters.

Lowe's conduct in this engagement shewed him to be a cowardly villain; for had he fought half as briskly as *Harris*, the Man-of-War could never have taken either of them. The *Greyhound* carried her Prize to *Rhode-Island*, which was looked upon to be of such signal service to the Colony, that in Council they resolved to compliment Peter Sulgard Captain, with the Freedom of their Corporation. They secured the prisoners under a strong guard in Jail, till a Court of Vice-Admiralty could be held for their Trials, which was on the 10th of July at *Newport*, lasting three days.

The Judges were *William Dummer*, Esq; Lieutenant Governor of the *Massachusets*, President; *Nathaniel Payne*, Esq; *John Lechmore*, Esq; Surveyor General; *John Valentine*, Esq; Advocate General; *Samuel Cranston*, Governor of *Rhode Island; John Menzies*, Esq; Judge of the Admiralty; *Richard Ward*, Esq; Registrar; and Mr. *Jahleet Brinton*, Provost Marshal. *Robert Auchmuta*, Esq, was appointed by the Court, Counsel for the prisoners here under mentioned.

Charles Harris, Captain, *William Blads, Daniel Hyde, Thomas Powel, jun., Stephen Munden, Thomas Hugget, William Read, Peter Kneeves, James Brinkley, Joseph Sound, William Shutfield, Edward Eaton, John Brown, Edward Lawson, Owen Rice, John Tomkins, John Fitzgerald, Abraham Lacy, Thomas Linester, Francis Leyton, John Walters*, Quartermaster, *William Jones, Charles Church, Thomas Hazel*, and *John Bright*, who were all executed the 19th of *July*, 1723, near *Newport* in *Rhode Island*; but *John Brown* and *Patrick Cunningham* were recommended to Mercy.

The eight following were found Not Guilty; *John Wilson, Henry Barnes, Thomas Jones, Joseph Switzer, Thomas Mumper*, Indian, *John Hencher*, Doctor, *John Fletcher*, and *Thomas Child*.

Instead of working repentance in *Lowe*, this deliverance made him ten times worse, vowing revenge upon all they should meet with for the future, which they executed upon Nathan Skiff, Master of a *Whale-fishing* Sloop, whom they whipt naked about the deck, and then cut off his ears, making his torture their sport.

At length being weary thereof, they shot him through the head, and sunk his vessel. Some days after, he took a fishing boat off of *Black* Island, and only cut off the master's head; but next day taking two Whale Boats near *Rhode* Island, he brutally killed one of the masters and cut off the ears of the other. From hence he went to *Newfoundland*, where he took 23 *French* Vessels, and mann'd one of them of 22 Guns with pirates; after which, they took and plundered 18 ships, some of which they destroyed.

The latter end of July, Lowe took a large ship called the *Merry Christmas*, and mounted her with 34 Guns, on which he goes aboard, taking the title of Admiral, and sails to the Western Islands, where he took a Brigantine manned with *English* and *Portugueze*, the latter of whom he hanged.

Afterwards Lowe went to the Coast of *Guinea*, but nothing happened till he came to *Sierra Leon*, in *Africa*, when he met with the *Delight*, which he took, mounting her with 16 Guns, and 60 men, appointing Spriggs Captain, and from whom two days after he separated.

In January after, he took a Ship called *Squirrel*, but what came of him afterwards we cannot tell.

CAPTAIN GEORGE LOWTHER, AND HIS CREW

CAPTAIN GEORGE LOWTHER, AND HIS CREW

GEORGE LOWTHER went second Mate on board the *Gambia Castle*, belonging to the *Royal African* Company, on board which was Captain Massey, with soldiers that he was to command under Colonel Whitney, whom were landed on *James* Island; but the Fort and Garrison not agreeing the Company soon after lost a Galley worth 10000*l*. by it.

Massey finding he must be over-ruled by the merchants, soon began to complain of their ill-treatment of his men in their allowance, saying he did not come to be a *Guinea* Slave; and that if they did not use him and his men better, he should take other measures.

At the same time, there happened a dispute between the Captain of the ship and Lowther, which very much contributing to Lowther's design: For Lowther finding himself neglected by the Captain, found means to ingratiate himself into the favour of the sailors, who, upon the Captain's going to punish him, swore, They would knock down the first man that should offer to lay hands on him; which Lowther improved to a general disaffection of the ship's Crew. Massey in the meantime, having contracted an intimacy with Lowther, they agreed to curb their enemies, and provide for themselves some other way; which the Captain perceiving, he goes on shore to the Governor and Factor, to consult what methods to take. But Lowther apprehending it was against him, he sent a letter in the same boat to Massey, advising him to repair on board, to put their project in execution.

Upon which Massey harangued the Soldiers, saying, *You that have a Mind to return to England,* may now do it; which they all agreed to. Then he went to the Governor's appartment, and took his bed, baggage, plate and furniture, believing the Governor would go with him, which he refused; however Massey came aboard with the Governor's son. After demolishing all the guns of the Fort, they weighed anchor, and fell down, but soon ran the ship aground; upon which Massey returns to the Fort, remounts the guns, and keeps garrison till the ship got clear. In the meantime Captain Russell got off but was not suffered to come on board, although he offered Lowther what terms he pleased. Next tide they got the ship afloat, having first nailed up and dismounted all the cannon. Then putting the Governor's son ashore, they put out to sea, when Lowther called upon the men, and told them, *It was Madness to think of returning to* England; *for what they had done, would be judged a Capital Offence;* and therefore, since they had a good ship under them, he proposed that they should seek their fortunes upon the Seas, as others had done before them, which they all agreed to, calling the ship *The Delivery,* and swore to stand by one another.

Lowther left the Fort the 13th of June, and on the 20th, near *Barbadoes,* he came up with a Brigantine, belonging to *Boston,* which he plundered, and then let go. After this he proceeded to *Hispaniola,* where he met with a *French* Sloop loaden with wine and brandy, on board whom Captain Massey went, pretending at first to be a merchant; but finding her to be a Ship of value, he told Monsieur, He must have it all without money. On board her, there was 30 casks of brandy, 5 hogsheads of wine, several pieces of chintz, and 70*l.* in money, all of which they took, only Lowther return'd the French Master five pounds again.

But this good harmony did not last long amongst them, Massey was uneasy, and resolved to leave them; which Lowther agreed to, giving him a Sloop he had just before taken, to go where he thought fit. Accordingly Massey goes aboard, with ten men, and comes in directly for *Jamaica,* where, putting a bold face on the matter, he informs Sir Nicholas Laws, the then Governor, how he had left Lowther the pirate, and of all that had been transacted before, adding, that he assisted him at the River *Gambia* only to save so many of His Majesty's subjects, and return to *England*.

Massey was well received, and, at his own report, he was sent on board the *Happy Sloop*, to cruise off *Hispaniola* for Lowther; but not meeting with him, he returned to *Jamaica*, and getting a Certificate, he came home to *England*, where, when he arrived, he writes to the *African* Company, relating the whole transaction of his voyage, but excuses it as an inadvertency, by his being ill-used; for which, if they would not forgive him, he begged to die like a soldier, and not be hanged like a dog. This not producing so favourable an answer as he expected, he went the next day to the Lord Chief Justice Chambers, and enquired, If there had been ever a Warrant granted and against one Captain Massey for Piracy. But being told, there was not, he said, He was the Man, and that the *African* Company would soon apply to my Lord for one, which if they did, he lodged in *Aldersgate street*, where the Officer might at any time find him. This the Clerk took down in writing, and a Warrant being soon granted, the Tipstaff went accordingly, and took him without any trouble.

But still there was no person to charge him, neither could they prove the letter to be his own hand-writing, till the Justice interrogated him, *Whether he did write the letter or not;* which he readily confessed, as also gave an ample account of the whole voyage, thereupon he was committed to *Newgate*, though soon after he was admitted out upon bail.

July the 5th, 1723, he was tried at the *Old-Baily* by a Court of Admiralty, when Captain Russell and others appeared against him: But he would have saved them all that trouble, for he confessed more than they knew, fixing the facts so firm upon himself, that he was found Guilty, received Sentence of Death, and was executed three weeks after at *Execution Dock*.

But to return to Lowther, whom Massey left cruising off of *Hispaniola*, who plying to the Windward near *Porto Rico*, took two sail, one was a small *Bristol Ship*, the other a *Spanish* Pirate, who had taken the *Bristol* Ship; which so provoked Lowther, that he threatened to put all the *Spaniards* to Death, for daring to intermeddle in his  Affairs: But at last he contented himself with burning both their ships; and the *Spaniards* getting away in their launch, they thought they were well off.

Afterwards he took a small Sloop from *St. Christophers*, which he manned; and carried with him to an island where they cleaned, and then going aboard, they sailed towards the Bay of *Honduras*, where they met with a small vessel with 13 Hands, of the same employment, under Captain Lowe, whom Lowther received as friends, inviting them, as they were few in number, to join their strength together;

which being accepted of, Lowther continued Captain, and Lowe was made Lieutenant, burning his own ship. Then coming into the Bay, they fell upon a ship of two hundred tons, called the *Greyhound*; against whom Lowther firing his guns, hoisted the piratical Colours, which Captain Edward bravely returned; but at length finding the Pirate too strong for him he yielded, and the Pirate came on board, and not only rifling the ship, but beat and cut the men in a cruel manner. In crusing about the Bay, they took several other vessels without any resistance, particularly a Sloop of 100 Tons, which they mounted with 8 carriages and 10 swivel guns. With this fleet, Lowther in the *Happy Delivery*, Lowe in the *Rhode Island* Sloop, Harris in *Hamilton's* Sloop, left the Bay, and came to *Port Mayo*, where they made preparations to careen, carrying ashore all their sails, to lay their plunder and stores in; but when they were busy at work, a body of the natives came down and attacked the Pirates unprepared, who were glad to fly to their Sloops, and leave them masters of the field, leaving the *Happy Delivery* behind them, contenting themselves with the *Ranger*, which had only 20 guns, and 8 swivels, taking all the men on board her, wherein they presently began to quarrel, laying the blame upon one another. Being very much in want of provisions, they got to the *West Indies*, May 1722, and near the Island of *Descada* took a Brigantine stored with provisions and necessaries, which put them in better temper. Then they watered and stood to the Northward, intending to visit the North Coast of *America*, and in Latitude

38, they took the *Rebecca* of *Boston*, at which time the Crews divided, Lowe with 44 Hands went on board the Brigantine, and Lowther with the same number, staid in the Sloop, separating that very night, being the 28th of May 1722.

Lowther cruised a pretty while among the Islands to no purpose, till at length he fell in with a *Martinico* Man, which proved a seasonable relief, he being reduced to great want of provisions, and after that a *Guinea* Man. After which they thought it time to clean, in order to prepare for new adventures; for which purpose they sailed to the Island of *Blanco*, which is a low Island 30 leagues from the main of *Spanish America*, where he unrigged his Sloop, sending his guns, rigging, and sails ashore, and putting his vessel upon the careen. But the *Eagle* Sloop of *Barbadoes*, coming near this Island, and seeing her, supposing her to be a Pirate, took the advantage of attacking her when unprepared, who immediately hoisted the *St. George's* Flag at her top-mast head to bid them defiance: But when they found the *Eagle* resolved to board them in good earnest, the Pirates cut their cable, and hawled the stern on shore, which obliged the *Eagle* to come to an anchor athwart the hawse, where they engaged them till they cried out for Quarters. At which time Lowther and 12 men made their escape, but they took the rest, and brought them to *Camena*, where the *Spanish* Governor condemned the Sloop to the captors, and sent 23 Hands to scour the bushes of *Blanco* for the Pirates, when they took 40; but could not find

Lowther, three men and a little boy. *John Churchill, Edward Mackonald, Nicholas Lewis, Rich. West, Sam Lavercot, Rob. White, John Shaw, And. Hunter, Jonathan Delve, Matthew Freeborn,* and *Henry Watson,* were hanged, *Roger Granger, Ralph Candem,* and *Robert Willis,* were acquitted. And Captain *Lowther,* it is said, afterwards shot himself, being found dead, and a pistol burst by his side.

CAPTAIN ANSTIS, AND HIS CREW

CAPTAIN ANSTIS,
AND HIS CREW

THOMAS ANSTIS shipped himself at *Providence*, in the Year 1718, aboard the *Buck* Sloop, and was one of the six that conspired together to get off with the vessel, along with Howel Davis, Dennis Topping, and Walter Kennedy, etc. I shall only observe, that this combination was the beginning of Captain Roberts's company, which afterwards proved so formidable, from whom Anstis separated the 18th of April, 1721, leaving his Commodore to pursue his adventures upon the Coasts of *Guinea*, whilst he returned to the *West Indies*, upon the same design.

About the middle of June, he met with one Captain Maiston, between *Hispaniola* and *Jamaica*, bound to *New-York*, from which he took all the wearing apparel, liquors and provisions, and six men. Afterwards he met with the *Irwin*, Captain Ross from *Cork*, on the Coast of *Martinico*, which ship had Colonel Doyly of

Montserrat on board, and his family, and 600 barrels of beef.

Afterwards they went into one of the Islands to clean, and thence proceeding towards *Bermudas*, they met with a stout ship called the *Morning Star*, bound from *Guinea* to *Carolina*, which they kept for their own use. Just after, they took a ship from *Barbadoes* bound to *New England*, from whence taking her guns, they mounted the *Morning Star* with 32 pieces of cannon, and 100 men, appointing John Fenn Captain: For Anstis was so in love with his own vessel, she being a good sailor, he made it his choice to stay in her, and let Fenn have the other ship. Though they were not sufficiently strong, yet being most new men, they could not agree, but resolving to break up company, sent a Petition to His Majesty by a Merchant Ship, expecting her Return at *Cuba*.

Here they staid about nine months; but not having provisions for above two, they were obliged to take what the Island afforded; which is many sorts of fish, particularly turtle; though they eat not a bit of bread, nor flesh meat, during their being on the Island.

They passed their time here in dancing, and other diversions, agreeable to these sort of folks. Among the rest, they appointed a mock Court of Judicature, to try one another for Piracy, and he that was a Criminal one day, was made a Judge another. I shall never forget one of their Trials, which for the curiosity of it, I shall relate. The Judge got up into a tree, having a dirty tarpaulin over his shoulders for a robe, and a Thrum Cap upon his head, with a large pair of spectacles upon his nose, and a monkey bearing up his train, with abundance of Officers attending him, with crows and hand-spikes instead of wands and tip-staves in their hands. Before whom the Criminals were brought out, making 1000 wry Faces; when the Attorney-General moved the Court, and said, An't please your Lordship, and you Gentlemen of the Jury, this fellow before you is a sad dog, a sad, a sad dog, and I hope your Lordship will order him to be hanged out of the way; he has committed Piracy upon the High Seas; nay, my Lord, that's not all; this fellow, this sad dog before you, has out-rid a hundred storms, and you know, my Lord, He *that's born to be hanged, will never be drowned.* Nor is this all, he has been guilty of worse villany than this, and that is of drinking of small beer; and your Lordship knows, there was never a sober fellow

but what was a rogue—My Lord, I should have said more, but your Lordship knows our rum is out, and how should a Man speak that has drunk a dram to-day.

Judge. Harkee me, Sirrah—you ill–looked dog. What have you to say why you may not be tucked up, and set a-sundrying like a scare-crow?—Are you Guilty, or not?

Prisoner. Not Guilty, an't please your Worship.

Judge. Not Guilty! say so again, and I will have you hanged without any Trial.

Prisoner. An't please your Worship's Honour, my Lord, I am as honest a fellow as ever went between stem and stern of a ship, and can hand, reef, steer, and clap two ends of a rope together, as well as e'er a He that ever crossed Salt-water; but I was taken by one *George Bradley* (the name of the Judge) a notorious Pirate, and a sad rogue as ever was hanged, and he forced me, an't please your Honour.

Judge. Answer me, Sirrah—how will you be tried?

Prisoner. By God and my country.

Judge. The Devil you will . . . Then, Gentlemen of the Jury, we have nothing to do but to proceed to Judgment.

Attorney-Gen. Right, my Lord; for if the fellow should be suffered to speak, he might clear himself; and that, you know, is an affront to the Court.

Prisoner. Pray, my Lord, I hope your Lordship will consider.

Judge. Consider!—How dare you talk of considering!—Sirrah, Sirrah, I have never considered in all my life.—I'll make it Treason to consider.

Pris. But I hope your Lordship will hear reason.

Judge. What have we to do with Reason ?—I would have you to know, Sirrah, we do not sit here to hear Reason—we go according to Law.—Is our dinner ready?

Attorney-General. Yes, my Lord.

Judge. Then harkee you rascal at the Bar, hear me, Sirrah, hear me. —You must be hanged for three reasons: *First*, because it is not fit that I should sit as Judge, and no-body to be hang'd: *Secondly*, You must be hang'd because you have a damn'd hanging Look: *Thirdly*, You must be hanged, because I am hungry. There's Law for you, ye dog; take him away, Goaler.

By this we may see how these fellows can jest upon things, the thoughts of which should make them tremble.

August 1722, they made ready the Brigantine, and came out to sea, where meeting their correspondent returning, and finding nothing done, they all agreed to ply their old trade. So they sailed with the ship and Brigantine to the Southward, where they ran the *Morning Star* upon the *Grand Carmanes*, and wrecked her; the next day Anstis went ashore to fetch the men off, who were all safe. Anstis had just time to get Captain Fenn, and a few others on board, before the *Hector* and *Adventure* came down upon him; but he got to sea, and one of the Men-of-War after him, keeping within gun-shot several hours, when the wind dying away, the Pirates got to their oars, and rowed for their lives.

The *Hector* landed her men, and took 40 of the *Morning Star's* Crew, without any resistance, they pretending they were glad of this opportunity; the rest hid themselves in the woods.

The Brigantine after her escape, sailed to an Island, near the Bay of *Honduras*, to clean, and in her way took a Sloop, Captain Durfey Commander, which they destroyed, but brought the men on board. While she was cleaning, Durfey conspired with some of the prisoners, to carry off the Brigantine but it being discovered, he and four or five more got ashore, with arms and ammunition; and when the Pirates' Canoe came in for water, seized the boat and men; upon which, Anstis sent another boat with 30 hand ashore; but Durfey gave them such a warm reception that they were glad to return back again.

In December 1722, Anstis left this place, taking in his cruise a good ship. He mounted her with 24 Guns and made Fenn Commander. From hence they went to the *Bahama* Islands, taking what they wanted.

As they were cleaning their ship the *Winchelsea* came down upon them, when most of them escaped to the woods; but Anstis having a light pair of heels, escaped in the Brigantine. Afterwards, some of the Company, being tired of this trade, shot Anstis in his Hammock, and put the rest in irons, and then carried the Brigantine to *Curacco*, a *Dutch* Settlement, where they were hanged, and those that delivered up the vessel acquitted. Fenn was soon after taken by the Man-of-War's men, straggling in the woods, with a few more, and carried to *Antegoa* and hanged. But some escaped among the negroes, and were never heard of since.

CAPTAIN JOHN PHILLIPS, AND HIS CREW

CAPTAIN JOHN PHILLIPS, AND HIS CREW

J OHN PHILLIPS was bred a carpenter, but sailing in a West Country ship to *Newfoundland*, was taken by Anstis, who soon persuaded him to join with him, making him Carpenter of the vessel, in which station he continued till they broke up at *Tobago*, when he came Home in a Sloop that was sunk in *Bristol* Channel. But he did not stay long in *England*; for hearing of some of his companions being taken in *Bristol* Gaol, he moved off to *Topsham*, and there shipped himself with one Captain Wadham for *Newfoundland*, where when the ship came he ran away, and hired himself a splitter in the Fishery for the season: but he soon combined with others in the Fishery, to go off with one of the vessels that lay in the Harbour, and turn Pirate, and accordingly fixed upon the 29th of August, 1713, at night; but of 16 men that promised five only were as good as their Word. Notwithstanding, Phillips was for pushing on, assuring them that they should soon increase their company. Hereupon they seized a vessel, and went out to sea, when they soon began to settle their Officers to prevent dispute, appointing, *John Phillips*, Captain; *John Nutt*, Navigator of the vessel; *James Sparks*, Gunner; *Thomas Fern*, Carpenter; and *William White* was only a private man among them.

Before they left the Banks, they took several small fishing vessels, out of which they took some more Hands, and then sailed to the *West-Indies*: Among those that were taken, was one John Rose Archer who having been a pirate under *Blackbeard* was made Quarter-Master to the company: They came off *Barbadoes* in October, and cruised about the Islands about three months, without meeting with a vessel, so that they were almost starved for want of provisions, when at length they fell in with a *Martinico* Man of 12 guns and 35 hands, upon which they hoisted the Black Flag and ran up along side of the Sloop, with piratical Colours flying, swearing, If they did not strike immediately, they must expect no quarters; which so frightened the *Frenchman*, that he never fired a gun. Having got this supply, they took her provisions, and four of her men.

Having occasion to clean their vessel, Phillips proposed *Tobago*; and just as they had done, a Man-of-War's boat came into the Harbour, the ship cruising to the Leeward of the Island; which was no sooner gone, but they warped out, and plied to the Windward for safety.

In a few days they took a Snow with a few Hands in it, on board of which they sent Fern the Carpenter, *William Smith*, *Philips Wood*, and *Taylor*; but Fern being dissatisfied at Archer's being preferred before him to be Quarter-Master, persuaded the rest to go off with the prize; but Phillips gave them chase, and coming up with them, shot Wood, and wounded Taylor in the leg; upon which the other two surrendered.

From *Tobago* they stood away to the Northward, and took a *Portugueze* bound for *Brazil*, and two or three Sloops for *Jamaica*, in one of which Fern endeavouring to go off, was killed by Phillips, as was also another man for the like attempt, which made all the others more fearful of discovering their Minds, dreading the villany of a few hardened wretches, who feared neither God nor Devil, as Phillips was often used blasphemously to say.

On the 25th of March, they took two ships from *Virginia*, the Master's name of one was *John Phillips*, the Pirate's Name-sake; of the other, *Robert Mortimer*, a stout young man. Phillips staid on board Mortimer's Ship, while they transported the crew to the Sloop, when Mortimer took up a handspike and struck Phillips over the head; but not knocking him down, he recovered and wounded Mortimer with his sword; and the other two Pirates who were on board, coming to Phillip's assistance they cut Mortimer to pieces, while his own two men stood and looked on. Out of the other *Virginia* Man, they took *Edward Cheesman*, a carpenter, to supply the Place of Fern, who being averse to that way of life, proposed to J. Philamore, who was ordered to row Cheesman on board Mortimer's ship, to overthrow their Piratical government; which from time to time, as occasion offered, they consulted how to do. The Pirates, in the mean time, robbed and plundered several ships and vessels, bending their course towards *Newfoundland*, where they designed to raise more men, and do all the mischief they could on the Banks, and in the harbours. Towards which country, Phillips making his way, took one Salter in a Sloop on the Isle of *Sables*, which he kept, and gave Mortimer's Ship to the Mate and crew; also a Schooner, one Chadwell Master, which they scuttled in order to sink: But Phillips understanding that she belonged to Mr. Menors of *Newfoundland*, with whose vessel they first went off a-Pirating, said, *We have done him injury enough already*, and so ordering his vessel to be repaired, returned her to the Master.

In the afternoon, they chased another vessel, whose Master was an Inward Light Man, named Dependence Ellery, who told Phillips he took him for a Pirate as soon as he saw him, otherwise he would not have given him the Trouble of chasing him so long. This so provoked Phillips and his Crew, that they made poor Dependence, for his Integrity, dance about the Ship till he was weary. After which they took 10 other ships and vessels; and on the 14th of April, they took a Sloop belonging to Cape *Anne*, Andrew Harradine Master; which looking upon to be more fit for their purpose, they came on board, keeping only the Master of her

Prisoner, and sending the crew away in Salter's vessel. Cheesman broke his mind to Harradine, to destroy the crew. Upon this, it was concluded to be 12 a Clock at Noon, when Cheesman leaves his workingtools on the deck, as if he had been going to use them, walks off. But perceiving some signs of fear in Harradine, he fetches his brandy bottle, and gives him and the rest a dram, saying, *Here's to our next Meeting;* then he talks to Nutt, in the mean while Philamore takes up an axe, while Cheesman and Harradine sieze Nutt by the collar, and toss him over the side of the vessel.

By this time the Boatswain was dead; for as soon as Philamore saw the Master laid hold on, he up with the axe, and cut off the Boatswain's head, which Noise soon brought the Captain upon Deck, whom Cheesman saluted with the blow of a mallet, which broke his jaw-bone, but did not knock him down; upon which Harradine came to the Carpenter's aid, when Sparks the Gunner interposing, Cheesman trips up his Heels, and flung him into the arms of Charles Ivemay, who at that moment threw him into the Sea; and at the same time Harradine throws Captain Phillips after him, bidding the Devil take them both. This done, Cheesman jumps from the deck into the Hold, to knock Archer on the head, when Harry Gyles came down after him, desired his Life might be spared; which being agreed to, he was made a Prisoner, and secured.

All being over, they altered their course from *Newfoundland* to *Boston*, where they arrived the 3rd of May, to the great joy of the Province, and on the 12th of May, a special Court of Admiralty was held for the Trial of these Pirates, when *John Philamore, Edward Cheesman, John Cobs, Henry Gyles, Charles Joymay, John Boatman,* and *Henry Payne,* were honourably acquitted; as also three *French* Men, *John Baptis, Peter Taffery,* and *Isaac Lassen,* as also three Negroes, *Pedro, Francisco,* and *Pierro. John Rose Archer,* the Quarter-Master, *William White, William Taylor,* and *William Phillips* were condemned; altho' the two latter got a Reprieve, and the two former, *Archer* and *White,* were executed the 2nd of *June* following.

CAPTAIN TEACH,
ALIAS BLACKBEARD

CAPTAIN TEACH

CAPTAIN TEACH, *ALIAS* BLACKBEARD

EDWARD TEACH was a *Bristol* Man, and had served many years in the late wars, in a Privateer fitted out from *Jamaica*, in which he had often distinguished himself for his boldness. He was never thought fit to be entrusted with any Command, till he went a-pirating in the Year 1716, when Captain Benjamin Hornigold put him into a Prize Sloop, with whom he kept company till Hornigold surrendered.

In 1727, Teach and Hornigold sailed from *Providence* for *America*, where, in their way, they took a vessel with above 100 Barrels of Flour, as also a Sloop from *Bermudas*, and a Ship bound to *Carolina*; from which they had a good plunder. After cleaning at *Virginia*, they returned to the *West-Indies*, and made Prize of a *French Guinea* Man bound to *Martinico*, which Teach was made Captain of; but Hornigold with his Sloop returned to *Providence*, and surrendered to mercy. Aboard the *French Guinea* Ship, Teach mounted 46 guns, and called her *Queen Anne's Revenge*. Not long after he fell in with the *Scarborough* Man-of-War, who, after a long fight finding she could do no good with Teach, left him, and returned to Barbadoes, while Teach sailed to *Spanish America*. In his way, he met with Major Bonnet a Gentleman, formerly of a good estate in *Barbadoes*, in a small Sloop with which he had turned Pirate: But Teach finding Bonnet knew nothing of the matter, took him into his own Ship, and put one Richards Captain in his room, telling the Major, *That he had not been us'd to the Fatigues of the Sea, he had better decline it, and take his pleasure aboard his Ship.* At *Turnissi* they took in fresh water; but seeing a Sloop coming in, they ran to meet her, which struck her sail, upon the sight of the Black Flag, to Teach, who took the Captain and his men aboard, and put Israel Hands to mann the Sloop: From thence they sailed to the Bay, where they found a ship and four Sloops. Teach hoisted his Black Colours, at the sight of which, the Captain and his men left the Ship, and ran into the woods. Teach's Quarter-Master, with some of his men, took possession of her, and Richards secured the Sloops: One of which they burnt, because she belonged to *Boston*, where some of his men had been hanged; but the others they let go after plundering them.

From hence they sailed to the *Grand Canaries*, then to the *Bahama* Wrecks, and then to *Carolina*, where they took a Brigantine and two Sloops, lying off the

Bar of *Charles Town*; as also a Ship bound for *London*, with some passengers aboard. The next day they took another vessel coming out, and two Pinks going in, and a Brigantine with negroes, in the Face of the Town; which put the inhabitants into a sad fright, being in no condition to help themselves.

Teach, alias *Blackbeard*, sent Richards along with Mr. Mark, one of the Prisoners, to demand a chest of medicines of the Governor, several of his men being sick aboard; threatening otherwise to burn the Ships, and destroy all the prisoners, among whom was Mr. Samuel Wrag, one of his Council. Altho' this went very much against the inhabitants, yet they were forced to comply with it to save the lives of the many souls had in his custody. So sending him a chest worth about 3 or 4 hundred Pounds, Richards went back safe to the ships with his booty; which as soon as *Blackbeard* had received, (for so I shall call him for the future) he let the ships and the prisoners go, having first taken 1500*l.* Sterling, and some provisions out of her. From thence they sailed to North *Carolina*, where he had thoughts of breaking up the company, and securing the money and the best of the effects for himself and friends. Accordingly he ran a-ground, as if it had been by accident, and calling Israel Hands to his assistance, he ran the Sloop ashore near the other, and so they were both lost. This done *Blackbeard* goes into the *Revenge* and maroons 17 men upon a desert island; where they must inevitably have perished, if Bonnet had not after taken them up.

Blackbeard goes straight to the Governor of *North Carolina*, with Twenty of his men, and pleads his Majesty's Pardon, and receives Certificates thereupon. He went to his Sloop which lay at *Okere-Cock* Inlet, and set out for Sea upon another expedition, steering his Ship towards *Bermudas*. Meeting with one or two *English Vessels* in his way, he robb'd them only of provisions for his present occasion; but meeting with a *French* Ship laden with sugar and cocoa, he brought her home with her cargoe to *North Carolina*, where the Governor and the Pirates shared the plunder. He had no sooner arrived there, but he and four of his men made affidavit, That they found the *French* Ship at Sea, without ever a Man on board; upon which she was condemned. The Governor had sixty hogheads of sugar for his dividend, his Secretary twenty, and the rest were shared amongst the other Pirates. And for fear the ship might be discovered by some that might come into the River, *Blackbeard*, under pretence that she was leaky, and might sink, obtained an order from the Governor to bring her out into the River, and burn her; which they did, and sunk her bottom.

The Sloops trading in the River, being so often pillaged by *Blackbeard*, consulted with the traders what course to take, knowing it was in vain to make any application to the Governor; therefore they sent a deputation to the Governor of *Virginia*, to sollicit a force from the Men-of-War to destroy this Pirate. Accordingly the Governor consulted with the Captains of the *Pearl* and *Lime* Men-of-War, which lay in *St. James's* River; whereupon it was agreed, That the Governor should have a couple of small Sloops, and they should be mann'd out of the Men of War, the Command of which was given to Mr. Robert Maynard, first Lieutenant of the *Pearl*. But before they sailed, it was agreed in Council, to offer a reward of 100 pounds *for any one that should take* Edward Teach, *commonly called* Blackbeard; *for every Lieutenant, Master, Quarter-Master, Boatswain, or Carpenter Twenty Pounds; For every inferior Officer, Fifteen Pounds; And for every Man taken on Board each Sloop, Ten Pounds.*

Upon this, the Lieutenant sailed from *James's* River in *Virginia*, the 17th of November, 1718, and the 21st in the evening came to *Okere-cock* Inlet, where he had fight of the Pirate: And altho' this Expedition was made with all the Secrecy imaginable, yet *Blackbeard* had notice of it from the Governor of North *Carolina* and his Secretary: But having heard several false reports before, he gave the less credit to this, till he saw the Sloops; and then he put himself in a Posture of defense, with his 25 men.

Lieutenant Maynard came to an anchor that night, because the Channel was so intricate that there was no getting in, in the dark. In the morning, coming within gunshot of the Pirate, he received his fire: whereupon the *Maynard* stood directly towards him, endeavouring to make a running fight. Maynard's men being most exposed, he lost twenty at one broadside; upon which he ordered his men under deck, and bid them get ready for close fighting upon the first signal. Then *Blackbeard's* men pour'd in grenadoes; after which, seeing no Hands aboard, he told his men they were all kill'd; *Let's jump in, and fall to Plunder:* Which they had no sooner done, but the Lieutenant and his men gave them as unwelcome a reception as ever they met with before. The Lieutenant and *Blackbeard* fired first at each other, and then they went to it sword in hand, whilst the men on each side were as warmly engaged as their Captains, until the vessel was all over blood. *Blackbeard* stood it till he had received above twenty wounds, five of them being shots, before he fell down dead. Eight of his fourteen men being kill'd, and the other six being much wounded, they call'd for quarters; which was granted, and then the Lieutenant attacked with equal bravery the men that remained in the Sloop and took them.

The Lieutenant caused *Blackbeard's* head to be cut off, and hung at the bowsprit end; with which he sailed to *Bath Town* to get his wounded men cured, and then began to rummage the Pirate Sloop, aboard which they found several Letters of Correspondence betwixt the Governor of *North Carolina*, his Secretary, and some Traders of *New York* and *Blackbeard*. Thereupon going to Bath Town in *North Carolina*, he seized in the Governors Store-house, the sixty hogsheads of sugar, and *Mr. Knight* his Secretary's 20, which was their dividend of the plunder taken in the French Ship before-mentioned.

After his men were a little recovered, he returned to the Men-of-War in *James's* River in *Virginia*, with *Blackbeard's* head hanging at his bowsprit, and 15 prisoners, 13 of whom were hanged, one of them being taken but the night before out of a trading Sloop: The other, not being in the fight, was taken at *Bath Town*, being just before disabled by *Blackbeard* in one of his drunken humours.

The night before he was killed, being ask'd if he should chance to be killed, whether his wife knew where his money was; he answered, *That no-body but himself and the Devil, knew where it was, and the longest Liver should take all.*

The Names of the Pirates killed in the engagement were *Edward Blackbeard*, Commander; *Philip Morton*, Gunner; *Garnet Gibbons*, Boatswain; *Owen Roberts*, Carpenter; *Thomas Miller*, Quarter-Master; *John Husk, Joseph Curtice, Joseph Brooks, Nath. Jackson.*

The following, except the two last, were hanged, viz.: *John Carnes, Jo. Brookes, jun., James Blake, John Gibbs, Thomas Gates, James White, Richard Styles, Cesar, Joseph Philip, James Robbins, John Martyn, Edward Salter, Stephen Daniel, Richard Greensarl, Israel Hands,* and *Samuel Odel.*

MAJOR STEDE BONNET,
AND HIS CREW

MAJOR STEDE BONNET

MAJOR STEDE BONNET,
AND HIS CREW

THE Major was a Gentleman of Fortune and Distinction in the Island of *Barbadoes*, who before his Piracy bore the character of a worthy honest *man*, and no-body could ever account for this his undertaking, for he wanted neither learning nor understanding. He fitted out a Sloop with ten guns and sixty men, which he named the *Revenge*, at his own expence, and sailed from *Barbadoes* for the Cape of *Virginia*, where he took the *Anne* from *Glasgow*, the *Turbet* from *Barbadoes*, the *Endeavour* from *Bristol*, the *Young* from *Leith*, and many others. From thence he went to *New York*, and there took a Sloop, and then stood in at *Gardiner's* Island where he bought provisions, and went off. August, 1717, he came off at the Bar of *South Carolina*, and took a Sloop and Brigantine, which they plundered, and then he dismissed the Brigantine, but took the Sloop with him to an Inlet in *North-Carolina*, where he careened, and set her on fire.

Afterwards he put to sea, but could not agree with the men what course to take; for the Major being no sailor, was obliged to submit to many things his men imposed upon him, when falling in with Edward Teach, alias *Blackbeard*, who was a good sailor, but a hardened villain, Bonnet's Crew joined with him, and put Bonnet aboard *Blackbeard's* Ship.

But *Blackbeard* losing his Ship at *Topsail* Inlet, surrendered to the King's Proclamation; when Bonnet re-assumed the command of his own Sloop, and sailed directly for *Bath* Town in *North-Carolina*, where he also surrenders himself, and receives a certificate. There getting a clearance for his Sloop, he pretended to sail for the Island of *St. Thomas*, to get the Emperor's Commission to go a-Privateering upon the *Spaniards*. But returning to *Topsail* Inlet, he found that *Blackbeard* and his gang were gone, with their effects; and that they had set on shore, on a small sandy island about a league from the continent, seventeen men, without any provisions, or vessel to escape. There they had been two nights and one day without any sustenance, when, to their inexpressible joy, they saw Major Bonnet, who had been informed of their being there by two of *Blackbeard's* crew, who had escaped to avoid his cruelty.

Then he steered his course towards *Virginia*, where meeting with a Pink having Provisions on board, and they being in want, he took out of her ten barrels of pork, and five hundredweight of bread, and gave her, in exchange, ten casks of rice, and an old cable.

Two days after they took a Sloop of sixty tons, from which they took two hogsheads of rum, and two of molasses, and then put in her eight men, to take care of the Prize; but they not liking her new acquaintance took the first opportunity to get off with her.

After this the Major threw off all restraint, and became a downright Pirate, by the name of Captain Thomas, taking and plundering all the vessels he met with. He took off Cape *Henry*, two Ships from *Virginia*, bound to *Glasgow*; the next day a small Sloop from *Virginia* bound to *Bermudas*; from which they took twenty barrels of pork, and gave her in return, two barrels of rice, and as much, molasses. The next day they took another *Virginia* man, bound to *Glasgow*, out of which they took two men, and a few small things, and gave her a barrel of pork, and another of bread. From thence they sailed to *Philadelphia*, where they took a Schooner coming from *North Carolina* to *Boston*, from which they took two men, and two dozen of calves skins, to make covers for guns. In the latitude of 32, off of *Delaware River*, near *Philadelphia*, they took two Snows bound to *Bristol*, from which they took money and goods to the value of two hundred pounds; as also a Sloop of sixty tons, from *Philadelphia* to *Barbadoes*, from which they took a few goods, and let her go. The 29th of July, they took a Sloop of fifty tons, bound from *Philadelphia* to *Barbadoes*, laden with provisions, which they kept; as also another of sixty tons, from *Antegoa* to *Philadelphia*, having on board, rum, molasses, sugar, cotton and indigo, to the value of five hundred pounds, all of which they kept. Then they left *Delaware* Bay, and sailed to Cape *Fear* River, where they staid almost two months to repair their Sloop, which proved very leaky, till news came to *Carolina* of a Pirate's Sloop, with her Prizes, being there a-careening.

Whereupon Colonel William Rhet offered to go with two Sloops to attack them; which being by the Governor and Council approved of, he was commissioned on board the *Henry*, with eight guns and seventy men, commanded by Captain John Masters; and the *Sea Nymph*, commanded by Captain Farier-Hall, with as many guns and men; both under the Direction of the Colonel, who went on board the *Henry* the 14th of *September*, and sailed from Charles Town to *Swillivant's* Island, in order to cruise: where he was informed, by a small ship from *Antegoa*, which in sight of the Bar, was taken and plundered by Charles Vane, in a Brigantine of sixteen guns, and a hundred men; that he had taken two Sloops, one Captain Dill, Master, from *Barbadoes*; the other Captain Thompson, from *Guinea*, with seventy negroes, which they put on board one Yeats his consort, being a small Sloop with twenty-five men, who being weary of this course of life, ran into *Edisto* River, and surrender'd to his Majesty's Pardon, by which the owners got their negroes again, and Yeats and his men had their certificates sign'd.

Vane cruised for some time thereabouts, in hopes to take Yeats, and be revenged on him; during which time, he took a ship bound to London, to whom he gave out, that he designed to go to the southward; which Colonel Rhet hearing, sailed over the Bar the 15th with the two Sloops, and went after the Pirate Vane; but not meeting with him, tack'd and stood for Cape *Fear*, according to his first Design; and on the 26th following he entered the River, where he saw Bonnet, and the three Sloops his Prizes, at anchor; but the Pilot running the Sloops a-ground, hindered their getting up that night. The Pirates seeing the Sloops, and not knowing who they were, mann'd three canoes, and sent them down to take them; but finding their mistake, Bonnet took all the men out of the Prizes to engage them. Colonel Rhet's Sloops the next morning getting under sail, stood for the Pirates, who designed only to make a running fight; but the Colonel getting upon his quarters, he edged in upon the shore, and ran his Sloop a-ground. The Colonel's Sloops were soon in the same condition: The *Henry* grounded within pistol-shot of the Pirate, on his bow; the other, right a-head of him, almost out of gun-shot, which made it of but very little use to the Colonel. By this time the Pirate had a very great advantage: For his Sloop lifted from Colonel Rhet's, which converted them all over; and the Colonel Sloop's lifting the same way, was much exposed for about five hours, whilst they lay a-ground. The Colonel's Sloop being first a-float, he got into deeper water, and after mending his rigging, he stood for the Pirate, to go directly on board him; which they prevented, by hoisting a flag of truce, and surrendering soon after. The Colonel lost in this action ten men, and had fourteen wounded. The *Sea Nymph* had two killed, and four wounded. Among the Pirates were none killed, and three were wounded. The next day the Colonel weighed from Cape *Fear*, and arrived at *Charles Town* the 3rd of *October*, to the no small joy of the people of *Carolina*.

There being no publick prison, Bonnet was committed into the custody of the marshal, and his men were kept at the Watch-house under a strict guard; a little before the trial, *David Harriot* the Master, and *Ignatius Rathe* Boatswain, the evidences, were removed from the Crew, to the Marshals house, from whence on the 24th *Bonnet* and *Harriott* made their escape; which as soon as the Governor heard of, he published a Proclamation, promising a reward of 700 pounds to any one that would take him, and also sent several boats with armed men in pursuit of him.

Bonnet stood to the northward, in a small vessel; but through stress of weather, and want of necessaries, he was forced to *Swillivant's* Island. Of which information being given to the Governor, he sent for Colonel Rhet, and desired him once more to go in pursuit of him; which the Colonel readily accepted of; and having got all things ready, went that night for *Swillivant's* Island, where, after a long search, he discovered them. After the Colonel's men had fired upon them, and killed Harriott, Bonnet immediately surrendered himself, and was, next morning, brought back to *Charles Town*, and confined under a strong guard till his trial, which was hastened for fear he should give them the slip again.

On the 28th of October, 1718, a Court of Vice-Admiralty was held at *Charles Town*, and, by several adjournments continued to the 12th of November following, by *Nicholas Trot*, Esq; Judge of the Vice-Admiralty, and Chief Judge of *Carolina*, and other Assistant Judges; where, after the King's Commission was read, and a Grand Jury sworn, *Judge Trot* gave them a learned Charge: And then the *Grand Jury* went out, and found the Bills; upon which, a *Petit-Jury* was sworn, and the following Persons were arraign'd and try'd.

Stede Bonnet, alias *Edwards*, alias *Thomas*, late of *Barbadoes*, Merchant.

Robert Tucker, late of *Jamaica*, Merchant.

Edward Robinson, late of *Newcastle*-upon-*Tine*, Mariner.

Neal Peterson, late of *Aberdeen*, Mariner.

William Scot, late of *Aberdeen*, Mariner.

William Eddy, alias *Neddy*, late of *Aberdeen*, Mariner.

Alexander Annand, late of *Jamaica*, Mariner.

George Rose, late of *Glasgow*, Mariner.

George Dubin, late of *Glasgow*, Mariner.

John Ridge, late of *London*, Mariner.

Matthew King, late of *Jamaica*, Mariner.

Daniel Perry, late of *Guernsey*, Mariner.

Henry Virgin, late of *Bristol*, Mariner.

James Rattle, alias *Robbins*, late of *London*, Merchant.

James Mullet, alias *Millet*, late of *London*, Mariner.

Thomas Price, late of *Bristol*, Mariner.

James Wilson, late of *Dublin*, Mariner.

John Lopez, late of *Oporto*, Mariner.

Zachariah Long, late of the Province of *Holland*, Mariner.

Job. Barley, late of *London*, Mariner.

John William Smith, late of *Charles* Town in *Carolina*, Mariner.

Thomas Carman, late of *Maidstone* in *Kent*, Mariner.

John Thomas, late of *Jamaica*, Mariner.

William Morrison, late of *Jamaica*, Mariner.

Samuel Booth, late of *Charles* Town, Mariner.

William Howet, late of *Jamaica*, Mariner.

John Kent, late of *North Carolina*, Mariner.

William Livres, alias *Evis*, late of *Carolina*, Mariner.

John Brierly, alias *Timberhead*, late of *Bath* Town in *North Carolina*, Mariner.

Robert Boyd, late of *Bath* Town in North *Carolina*, Mariner.

Thomas Nicholas, late of *London*, Mariner.

Rowland Sharp, late of *Bath* Town, Mariner.

Jonathan Clark, late of *Charles* Town, Mariner.

Thomas Gerrard, late of *Antegoa*, Mariner.

All of whom, except the four last, were found Guilty, and received Sentence of Death, upon two Indictments, for Robbing upon the High Sea the *Francis, Peter Manwaring*, Commander; and for seizing, in a Piratical Manner, the Sloop *Fortune, Thomas Read*, Commander: To which they all pleaded Not Guilty, except *James Wilson* and *John Levit*, who pleaded Guilty to both Indictments, and *Daniel Piercy* to one only. *Bonnet* moved to go through both the Indictments at once; but the Court overruling it, he was found Guilty of one, and retracted his Plea to the other. They made but little Defence, pretending they were taken off a *Maroon* Shore, and were shipped with Major Bonnet to go to *St. Thomas's*, but wanting provisions they were obliged to do what they did; and the Major himself pretended it was *Necessity* and not *Inclination* that compelled them to do it. But that not appearing, they having all shared ten or eleven pounds a man, except the four last, they were all found Guilty. After which the Judge set forth the enormity of their Crimes: And then pronounced Sentence of Death upon the persons aforesaid, except Major *Bonnet*, who not being brought back in time, was not tried till the 10th of November; and being then also found Guilty, he received Sentence in like manner as the others; before whom Judge *Trot* made an excellent speech, saying afterwards.

And now, having discharged my Duty as a Christian, I must do my Office as a Judge, which is You the said Stede Bonnet *shall go from hence, to the Place from whence you came, and from thence to the Place of Execution, where you shall be hanged by the Neck till you are dead.*

CAPTAIN WILLIAM KID

CAPTAIN WILLIAM KID

CAPTAIN WILLIAM KID

WE are now going to give an account of one whose name is better known in *England*, than most of those whose histories we have already related; the person we mean is Captain Kid, whose public Trial and Execution here, rendered him the subject of all conversation.

In the beginning of King *William's* War, Captain Kid commanded a Privateer in the *West-Indies*, and by several adventurous actions acquired the reputation of a brave man, as well as an experienced seaman. About this time the Pirates were very troublesome in those parts, wherefore Captain Kid was recommended by the Lord Bellamont, then Governor of *Barbadoes*, as well as by several other persons, to the Government here, as a person very fit to be entrusted with the command of a Government Ship, and to be employed in cruising upon the Pirates, as knowing those Seas perfectly well, and being acquainted with their lurking places; but what reasons governed the politics of those times, I cannot tell, but this proposal met with no encouragement here, though it is certain it would have been of great consequence to the subject, our merchants suffering incredible damages by those robbers.

Upon this neglect the Lord Bellamont, and some others who knew what great captures had been made by the Pirates, and what a prodigious wealth must be in their possession, were tempted to fit out a ship at their own private charge, and to give the command of it to Captain Kid; and to give the thing a greater reputation, as well as to keep their seamen under the better command, they procured the King's Commission for the said Captain Kid.

Captain Kid had also another Commission, which was called a Commission of Reprisals; for it being then War time, this Commission was to justify him in the taking of *French* Merchant Ships, in case he should meet with any. He sail'd out of *Plymouth* in May 1696, in the *Adventure* Galley of thirty guns, and eighty men; the place he first designed for was *New York*; in his voyage thither he took a French *Banker*, but this was no Act of Piracy, he having a Commission for that purpose, as we have just observed.

When he arrived at *New York* he put up Articles for engaging more Hands, it being necessary to his Ship's crew, since he proposed to deal with a desperate enemy: The terms he offered were, that every man should have a share of what was taken, reserving for himself and Owners forty shares. Upon this encouragement he soon increas'd his company to a hundred and fifty five men.

With this company he first sail'd for *Maderas*, where he took in wine and some other necessaries; from thence he proceeded to *Bonavist*, one of the *Cape de Verd Islands*, to furnish the ship with salt, and from thence went immediately to *St. Jago*, another of the *Cape de Verd Islands*, in order to stock himself with provisions. When all this was done, he bent his course to *Madagascar*, the known rendezvous of Pirates; in this way he fell in with Captain Warren, Commodore of three Men-of-War; he acquainted them with his design, kept them company two or three days, and then leaving them, made the best way for *Madagascar*, where he arrived in *February* 1696, just nine months from his departure from *Plymouth*.

It does not appear all this while that he had the least design of turning Pirate; for near *Mahala* and *Joanna* both he met with several *Indian* ships richly laden, to which he did not offer the least violence, tho' he was strong enough to have done what he pleas'd with them; and the first outrage or depredation I find he committed upon mankind,  was after his repairing his ship, and leaving *Joanna*; he touch'd at a place call'd *Mabbee*, upon the *Red Sea*, where he took some *Guinea* Corn from the natives, by force.

After this he sail'd to *Bab's Key*, a Place upon a little Island at the entrance of the *Red Sea*; here it was that he first began to open himself to his ship's company, and let them understand that he intended to change his measures; for, happening to talk of the *Moca* Fleet, which was to sail that way, he said *We have been unsuccessful hitherto, but courage, my Boys, we'll make our fortunes out of this Fleet:* And finding that none of them appear'd averse to it, he ordered a boat out, well mann'd, to go upon the coast to make discoveries, commanding them to take a prisoner and bring to him, or get intelligence any way they could. The boat return'd in a few days, bringing him word, that they saw fourteen or fifteen ships ready to sail, some with *English*, some with *Dutch*, and some with *Moorish* Colours. He therefore order'd a man continually to watch at the mast-head, least this Fleet should go by them; and about four days after, towards evening, it appear'd in sight, being convoy'd by one *English* and one *Dutch* Man-of-War. Kid soon fell in with them, and getting into the midst of them, fir'd at a *Moorish* ship which was next him; but the Men-of-War taking the Alarm, bore down upon Kid, and firing upon him, obliged him to sheer off, he not being strong enough to contend with them. Now he had begun hostilities, he resolv'd to go on, and therefore he went and cruis'd along the coast of *Malabar*; the first Prize he met was a small vessel belonging to *Aden*, the vessel was *Moorish*, and the Owners were *Moorish* Merchants, but the Master was an *Englishman*, his name was

Parker. Kid forc'd him and a *Portugueze* that was call'd Don Antonio, which were all the *Europeans* on board, to take on with them; the first he design'd as a pilot, and the last as an interpreter. He also used the men very cruelly, causing them to be hoisted up by the arms, and drubb'd with a naked cutlass, to force them to discover whether they had money on board, and where it lay; but as they had neither gold nor silver on board, he got nothing by his cruelty; however, he took from them a bale of pepper, and a bale of coffee, and so let them go.

Soon after this he came up with a *Moorish* Ship, the Master whereof was a *Dutchman*, call'd Schipper Mitchel, and chased her under *French* Colours, which they observing, hoisted *French* Colours too: When he came up with her, he hail'd her in *French*, and they having a *Frenchman* on board, answer'd him in the same language; upon which he order'd them to send their boat on board; they were oblig'd to do so, and having examin'd who they were, and from whence they came; he ask'd the Frenchman, who was a passenger, if he had a French pass for himself? The *Frenchman* gave him to understand that he had. Then he told the *Frenchman* he must pass for Captain, *and by God*, says he, *you are the Captain*: The *Frenchman* durst not refuse doing as he would have him: The meaning of this was, that he would seize the Ship as fair Prize, and as if she belonged to *French* Subjects, according to a commission he had for that purpose; tho', one would think, after what he had already done, that he need not have recourse to a quibble to give his actions a colour.

In short, he took the cargoe and sold it some time after, yet still he seem'd to have some fears upon him least these proceedings should have a bad end; for, coming up with a *Dutch* Ship some time, when his men thought of nothing but attacking her, Kid oppos'd it; upon which a mutiny arose, and the majority being for taking the said ship, and arming themselves to man the boat to go and seize her, he told them, such as did, never should come on board him again; which put an end to the design, so that he kept company with the said ship some time, without offering her any violence: However, this dispute was the occasion of an accident, upon which an indictment was afterwards grounded against Kid; for Moor, the Gunner, being one day upon deck, and talking with Kid about the said *Dutch* Ship, some words arose betwixt them, and Moor told Kid, that he had ruin'd them all; upon which, Kid, calling him *Dog*, took up a bucket and struck him with it, which breaking his skull, he died the next day.

But Kid's penitential fit did not last long, for coasting along *Malabar*, he met with a great number of boats, all which he plunder'd. Upon the same Coast he also lit upon a *Portugueze* Ship, which he kept possession of a week, and then having taking out of her some chests of *Indian* goods, thirty jars of butter, and some wax, iron, and a hundred bags of rice, he let her go.

The *Adventure* Galley was now so old and leaky, that they were forced to keep two pumps continually going, wherefore Kid shifted all the guns and tackle out of her into the *Queda* Merchant, intending her for his Man-of-War; and as he had divided the Money before, he now made a division of the remainder of the cargo: Soon after which, the greatest part of the company left him, some going on board Captain Culliford, and others absconding in the Country, so that he had not above forty men left.

He put to sea and happened to touch at *Amboyna*, one of the *Dutch* Spice Islands, where he was told, that the news of his actions had reach'd *England*, and that he was there declared a Pirate.

The truth on't is, his Piracies so alarmed our Merchants, that some motions were made in Parliament, to enquire into the commission that was given him, and the persons who fitted him out: These proceedings seem'd to lean a little hard upon the Lord Bellamont, who thought himself so much touch'd thereby, that he published a Justification of himself in a pamphlet after Kid's execution. In the mean time, it was thought advisable, to publish a Proclamation, offering the King's free Pardon to all such Pirates as should voluntarily surrender themselves, whatever Piracies they had been guilty of at any time, before the last day of April, 1699—That is to say, for all Piracies committed Eastward of the *Cape of Good* Hope, to the Longitude and Meridian of *Socatora*, and *Cape Camorin*. In which Proclamation, Avery and Kid were excepted by Name.

When Kid left *Amboyna* he knew nothing of this Proclamation, for certainly had he had notice of his being excepted in it, he would not have been so infatuated, to run himself into the very jaws of danger; but relying upon his interest with the Lord Bellamont, and fancying, that a *French* Pass or two he found on board some of the ships he took, would serve to countenance the matter, and that part of the booty he got would gain him new friends—I say, all these things made him flatter himself that all would be hushed, and that justice would but wink at him. Wherefor he sail'd directly for *New York*, where he was no sooner arrived, but by the Lord Bellamont's orders, he was secured with all his papers and effects. Many of his fellow-adventurers who had forsook him at *Madagascar*, came over from thence passengers, some to *New England* and some to *Jersey*; where hearing of the King's Proclamation for pardoning of Pirates, they surrendered themselves to the Governor of those places: At first they were admitted to bail, but soon after were laid in strict confinement, where they were kept for some time, till an opportunity happened of sending them with their Captain over to *England* to be tried.

Accordingly a Sessions of Admiralty being held at the *Old Baily*, in May, 1701, *Captain Kid, Nicholas Churchill, James How, Robert Lumley, William Jenkins,*

Gabriel Loff, Hugh Parrot, Richard Barlicorn, Abel Owens, and *Darby Mullins*, were arraingn'd for Piracy and Robbery on the High Seas, and all found guilty, except three; these were *Robert Lumley, William Jenkins*, and *Richard Barlicorn*, who proving themselves to be apprentices to some of the officers of the ship, and producing their Indentures in Court, were acquitted.

Kid was tried upon an indictment of Murder also, *viz.* for killing *Moor* the Gunner, and found guilty of the same. *Nicholas Churchill* and *James How* pleaded the King's Pardon, as having surrendered themselves within the time limited in the Proclamation, and Colonel *Bass*, Governor of *West Jersey*, to whom they surrendered, being in Court, and called upon, proved the same; however, this plea was over-ruled by the Court, because there being four Commissioners named in the Proclamation, it was adjudged no other person was qualified to receive their surrender, and that they could not be intitled to the benefit.

As to Captain Kid's Defence, he insisted much upon his own innocence, and the villany of his men; he said he went out in a laudable employment and had no occasion, being then in good circumstances, to go a-Pirating; that the men often mutinied against him, and did as they pleas'd; that he was threatened to be shot in his cabin, and that ninety five left him at one time, and set fire to his boat, so that he was disabled from bringing his ship home, or the Prizes he took, to have them regularly condemn'd, which he said were taken by virtue of a commission under the broad seal, they having *French* Passes—The Captain called one Col. *Hewson* to his Reputation, who gave him an extraordinary character, and declared to the Court, that he had served under his command, and been in two engagements with him against the *French*, in which he fought as well as any man he ever saw; that there were only *Kid's* Ship and his own against Monsieur *du Cass*, who commanded a squadron of six sail, and they got the better of him, but this being several years before the facts mentioned in the Indictment were committed, prov'd of no manner of service to the Prisoner on his Trial.

As to the friendship shown to *Culliford*, a notorious Pirate, *Kid* denied, and said, he intended to have taken him, but his men being a parcel of rogues and villains refused to stand by him, and several of them ran away from his ship to the said Pirate.—But the evidence being full and particular against him, he was found Guilty as before mentioned.

When *Kid* was asked what he had to say why Sentence should not pass against him, he answered, That *he had nothing to say, but that he had been sworn against by perjured wicked People.* And when Sentence was pronounced, he said, *My Lord it is a very hard Sentence. For my part I am the innocentest Person of them all, only I have been sworn against by perjured Persons.*

Wherefore about a week after, Capt. *Kid, Nicholas Churchill, James How, Gabriel Loff, Hugh Parrot, Abel Owen, and Darby Mullins,* were executed at *Execution*

Dock, and afterwards hung up in chains, at some distance from each other, down the river, where their bodies hung exposed for many years.

CAPTAIN EDWARD ENGLAND, AND HIS CREW

CAPTAIN EDWARD ENGLAND

CAPTAIN EDWARD ENGLAND,
AND HIS CREW

EDWARD ENGLAND went Mate of a Sloop that sailed out of *Jamaica*, and was taken by Winter, a Pirate, from whom he had the Command of a Sloop just before their Settlement at *Providence*. The man was brave and good natured, and far from being cruel, as most of them are; and would not have committed such barbarous actions as he did, had not his comrades compelled him to it.

He sailed to the Coast of *Africa*, after the Island of *Providence* was inhabited by the *English*. In his Passage he took several Ships, particularly the *Cadogan* Snow belonging to *Bristol*, one Skinner Master, who was murdered by those very men who had formerly served under him, upon a quarrel that happened between Skinner and them, about their wages: He shipped them on board a Man-of-War, from whence they deserted, and went on board a ship in the *West-Indies*, where they were taken by a pirate, and brought to *Providence*, and then they sailed with Captain England a-Pirating.

As soon as *Skinner* came on board, he saw his old Boatswain, who said, *Ah! Captain Skinner is it you, I am much in your Debt, and now I shall pay you in your own Coin.* These words put the Captain in a panic Fear: And indeed he had Reason enough to be afraid, for they immediately seized him, bound him to the Windlass, pelted him with glass bottles, afterwards whipt him about the deck, and then said, because he had been a good Master, he should have an easy Death, and so shot him through the head; the vessel and her cargoe being given to *Howel Davis*.

After this *England* went into an *Harbour* to clean his Ship, and also fitted up the *Peterborough*, which he called the *Victory*. Then putting out to sea, they sailed for the *East-Indies*, and took *Madagascar*, by the Way. From thence, after taking in water and provisions, they went for *Malabar*, in the Empire of the *Mogul*. Here they took several *Indian* Vessels, and one *European*, a *Dutch* Ship, which they exchanged for one of their own, and then came back to *Madagascar*, were they sent several Hands on shore to kill venison, and then resolved to seek out for the remains of Avery's Crew; but returning without success, they being settled on the other side, they stay'd no longer than till they had cleaned their ships, and then sailed to *Juanna*.

In the Year 1720, the *Bombay* Fleet, consisting of four *Grabs*, the *London Chandois*, and some other ships, carried 1000 men to bombard and batter *Gapra*, a fort belonging to *Angria*, on the *Malabar* Coast; which they not being able to do, fell in with the Pirates, in their return to *Bombay*: But Captain Upton the Commodore, having no orders, would not engage them; which so provoked the Governor, for missing so favourable an opportunity of cutting the Pirates all off, that he gave the command to Captain Mackra, with orders to fight them wherever he met with them.

But the Pirates proceeded to the southward, and took a small ship out of *Orincro* Road, with a *Dutch* and two *Portugueze* Men on board, one of which they sent to the Captain, to inform him, that if he would supply them with provisions and water he should have his ship again. But the Master would not agree to it; thereupon they sent other persons ashore, and swore he should be the last man they would give quarter to, and so put directly for *Laccadeva* Island, and arrived there in three days. But being informed by a *Menchew*, there was no anchor-ground there, they went to the next Island, called *Melincha*, whence they were driven by a storm, leaving behind them a hundred people, and all their water-casks: But in a week's time, they regained the island, took their people on board, and filled the water-casks. Provisions being scarce, they resolved to visit the *Dutch* at *Cochin*, and after three days sail, arrived off of *Tellechery*, where they took a small vessel belonging to Governor Adams; who giving an account of Captain Mackra's fitting out against them, put them into a grievous passion.

Afterward they arrived at *Mauritius*, where they refitted the *Victory*, and then sailed the 5th of April for *Madagascar*, but called first at the Island *Mascarine*, at which they found a *Portugueze* ship of seventy guns at anchor, disabled by a violent storm, so that they easily became a Prize to the Pirates. She had on board the *Conde Ereceira* Vice-Roy of *Goa*, also they found on board her, in diamonds only, to the value of four millions of Dollars. They made the Vice-Roy a prisoner; but in consideration of his losses, accepted of a ransom of 2000 dollars and then set him and his followers ashore. Learning that an *Ostender* was on the leeward of that Island, they sailed and took her, and sent her to *Madagascar* with news of their success, where they followed themselves soon after, with two hundred *Mozambique* Negroes in the *Portugueze* Ship.

When Taylor came with the *Portugueze* Prize to *Madagascar*, they found that the *Ostender* had made his men drunk, and seized his ship, which they carried to the *Mozambique*; from thence the Governor ordered her to *Goa*. But the Pirates staid and clean'd the *Cassandra*, and divided very great plunder. Some, who thought they had got enough, staid at *Madagascar*, and the rest, having no occasion for two ships, burnt the *Victory*, she being leaky, and went on board the *Cassandra*, under the Command of Captain Taylor, designing to go for *Cochin* to dispose of his diamonds, amongst his old Friends the *Dutch*, and also to avoid the dangers of the Men-of-War that were in pursuit of them. But as he was preparing to sail, and heard of four Men-of-War coming after him; therefore he altered his mind, and sailed for the Main of *Africa*, and put in at *Delagoa*: But the Pirates were surprized in the evening with some shot from the shore. They took it for a desert shore, but it proved otherwise; for a few months before, the *Dutch East India Company* had settled one hundred men upon it, who, not being supplied with necessaries, were reduced to about sixteen; whom Taylor, upon their humble petition took aboard, and they all became Pirates with him.

Here they stayed about four months, careened their ships, and left *Delagoa* the latter end of *December*: But not agreeing among themselves, they parted those who were weary of that sort of life, went on board the *Portugueze* Prize, and sailed for *Madagascar*; the others went on board the *Cassandra*, and sailed for the *Spanish West Indies*. The *Mermaid* Man-of-War, which was a convoy to some Merchant-men, about 30 leagues distance, would have gone to attack them, had not the Merchants, whom he had the care of, declar'd their protection was of more service than destroying the Pirates; and so he was oblig'd to be content with only dispatching the news of it to *Jamaica*. This brought down the *Lanceston*, though it was a day or two too late, for they had just before surrendered, with all their riches, to the Governor of *Porto-Bello*, where they now live upon their Spoils, saying, others would have done as much, had they had the same opportunity; swearing,

That whatever Robberies they had committed they are not the only Rogues in the World; for that the South-Sea* did more Mischief in one Year, than they were able to do in their whole Lives.

* The South-Sea Bubble.

CAPTAIN JOHN GOW, *ALIAS* SMITH, AND HIS CREW

CAPTAIN JOHN GOW

CAPTAIN JOHN GOW, *ALIAS* SMITH, AND HIS CREW

JOHN GOW, alias *Smith*, was born at a place called *Caristoun*, in the *Orkney* Islands, and was brought up a sailor from his youth, having served on board several Men-of-War, and last of all on board the *Suffolk*, along with T. Swan, who was engaged with him in the conspiracy to murder Captain Ferneau, and seize the ship and cargoe, as they went off the *Texel*, but they were prevented by James Belvin, who was led into the secret and discovered it. Captain Ferneau taking little notice of it, contented himself with turning off Swan, and preferred Gow to be second Mate and Gunner.

They sailed on board the *George* Galley, August the 1st, 1724, from the *Texel* to *Santa Cruz*, having 15000*l* on board, when Gow designed to have seized the Ship as they went out, but could not get a party strong enough to join with him, till he worked up a misunderstanding between the Captain and part of the crew, concerning the provisions of the ship, particularly *Winter, Peterson,* and *Mc.Cawley,* who came upon the Quarter-Deck, in presence of the Owners, just before they sailed, and made a long complaint against the Captain; who assured them that if there was any wrong done them, it was not by his consent; and that he would enquire into it as soon as they had unmoored the ship.

About eight a clock at night, Captain Ferneau, as usual, called them up to prayers in the great Cabin, and then set the watch, and went to sleep, little thinking his end was so near, when Winter, Rawlisson, and Melvin, begun the scene of blood, Gow lying snug in his hammock, as if he knew nothing of the matter, till he saw whether the villany would succeed, or not. Winter cut the Doctor's throat as he was asleep in his hammock, and then went up to Melvin and Rawlisson, who in the mean time had seized the Captain and cut his throat also, but not touching the windpipe, Gow stept up and shot him with a brace of bullets, and then threw him over-board. *Mc.Cawley* cut *Stephen Algiers* the Clerk's throat, as he lay in the hammock, and *Williams* shot him dead afterwards. *Peterson* cut the throat of *Bonaventure Jelphs*, the Chief Mate; and *Michael Moor*, at the Command of *Williams*, shot him.

After this Williams came upon the Quarter-Deck, and saluted Gow with Captain Ferneau's sword, first striking it upon one of the guns, and saying, *Welcome*

Captain Gow, *welcome to your new Command.* After which, Gow told the men, That if any of them durst murmur or cabal together, they must expect to meet with the same Fate; and then calling a Council, they agreed to go, *Upon the Account*, as they called it.

They called the ship the *Revenge*, and mounted six more of her guns, she being able to carry four and twenty in all. But instead of going to *Genoa* as intended, they sailed for the coasts of *Spain* and *Portugal*, in hopes of getting a ship laden with wine, to keep up their spirits; but all was alike they met with; and instead of wine, they contented themselves with fish, which they took out of a ship called the *Delight* of Poole, Thomas Wise, Master, bound from *New-England* to *Cadiz*, out of which they took the men, and what they wanted, and then sunk the Ship, to prevent their being discovered to the *English* Men-of-War who lay in the *Straights*.

On the 18th of December, they took the *Snow-Galley*, out of which Crew they kept Rob, and discharged the Captain and the rest of the men, after having plundered the Ship of the arms, ammunition, cloth, provisions, sails, anchors, cables, and then let her go.

By this time, they were got a great way to the southward; and being in want of water as well as wind, they agreed to go to *Maderas*, which Island they made in two days, cruising about it near a week, expecting some vessel to come in or come out; but the Country discovering what they were, they were disappointed in their attempts. Then they stood away for *Porto Santa*, where they put up *British* Colours, and sent their Boat ashore with a compliment to the Governor, desiring leave to water, and buy some refreshments; which he readily agreed to, and went with them to pay the *English* Captain a visit, who received him in a very grand Manner. But the refreshments not coming as expected, he at length told him he was his Prisoner, and must remain so till the provisions were come on board, which was not till next day, when Gow discharged him, giving him three Cerons of Bees-wax, and three Guns at his going away.

Having now got provisions, they agreed to return to the Coasts of *Spain* and *Portugal*; where they had not been above two days, before they met with the *Batchelor*, Benjamin Cross Master, from *New-England* bound to *Cadiz*; out of which they took Cross and his men, and gave the Ship to Captain Wise, as also 24 Cerons of Bees-wax to him and his mate, and to his four men 8 Cerons. After this they took a *French* Ship from *Cadiz*, loaded with wine, oil, and fruit, which was what they wanted, and manned her with their own men, taking on board the *Revenge* the *French* Master, and his 12 men, and most Part of the cargoe, with five guns and their carriages, ammunition, small arms, and sails, and gave the ship to Somerville, Captain of the *Snow Galley;* and to Captain Cross the *New-English* Man, to who they gave half the ship and cargoe and Somerville had all his men, but Alexander Rob, whom they detained, and who was executed in 1725, for engaging along with them.

Soon after they saw a large ship to the windward bearing down upon them, which at first they thought to have been a *Portugueze* Man-of-War; but they found afterwards, it was a *French* Merchant Ship coming home from the *West-Indies*, which not fearing them, came on to the windward. Gow perceiving she was a Ship of great strength, called all his men together, telling them they had a great many prisoners on board, and that he could not trust many of his own men; besides, six of his best Hands were on board the other Ship, therefore he advised them not to meddle with her, she being far superior in Force. This so exasperated Williams, that he demanded of Gow to give his orders for fighting; but he, by the advice of the whole crew, declined it; whereupon Williams snapt his pistol at his Face; which not going off, made him still madder. Winter and Peterson standing by him fired each a Pistol at Williams, one shooting him through the arm, and the other in the belly; at which he fell, and they believing he was killed, were going to throw him overboard, when he leapt up, and ran into the Powder-Room, with his pistol cocked in his hand, swearing he would blow them all up; which he had certainly done, had they not prevented him that very moment, he having opened the scuttle to do it.

They immediately put him in irons, and hand-cuffed him, and then put him between decks, in a place prepared for prisoners.

Two days after this, they took the *Triumvirate*, a *Bristol* Sloop, Joel Davis Master, bound from

Newfoundland to *Oporto*, with fish; from whence they took all her provisions, arms, sails, and two of her men, and then let her go with the rest, and all her cargoe. Not knowing what to do with Williams, they resolved to put him on board them, and send him away, for fear of further danger, ordering the Master to put him on board the first *English* man of War he should meet with, to hang him for Piracy; which when Williams found they were resolved to do, he made all the submission he was able to Captain Gow, begging for pardon, knowing if he was carried to *Lisbon* he should meet with his deserts. But all his entreaties would not do, he was brought up double fettered, when he begged they would throw him into the sea, and drown him, rather than give him up to be hanged in chains, which he knew he deserved from the *Portugueze* as well as *English*. This made many of them begin to relent and pity him; but considering his savage disposition, they knew there was no safety to keep him on board, and so resolved to let him go, and give him a hearty curse at parting, wishing him a safe voyage to the gallows, not dreaming that they themselves should accompany him.

The *Bristol* Captain obeyed their orders, and as soon as he came to *Lisbon* put him on board the *Argyle* man of War, Captain Bowler Commander, who brought him home not above three days before Gow and his Crew came to keep him company.

In the middle of last January, they arrived at *Caristoun* in the Isles of *Orkney*, when Gow gave them instructions, what account they should give of themselves to the people of the country, to avoid suspicion. But now began their misfortunes, for several of their men began to think of making their escape, the first was one Read, who took an opportunity to get away when the boat went ashore, who went to a farm-house which lay under a hill where he hired a horse and rode to *Kirkwall*, a market town about twelve miles off, where he informed them what they were; whereupon they raised the Country to defend themselves. The Pirates soon hearing what was done, ten more of them went away with the longboat, making the best of their way for *Scotland*, who were some time after taken in the *Frith* of *Edinburgh*, and made Prisoners.

This so provoked Gow, that he resolved to plunder the Country, be the consequence what it would, and in order thereto, he sent Belvin his Boatswain, with Rob and Four more, to Mr. Honnyman's house, the Sheriff, who not being at home, his Servants let them in, not suspecting their design. They immediately fell to work, but Mr. Honnyman's Daughter had the presence of mind to hide the money in a tub of feathers, till she found an opportunity to carry it away, by the contrivance of Alexander Rob, who was placed centinel at the door. But when the Boatswain found the treasure was gone, Gow having before told them where it lay, he swore he would burn the house, and all that was in it, which the young Lady hearing, she runs to the Charter-room where the Treasure lay, and threw it out of the window, jumping herself after. However, they plundered the house of about fifty pounds, and some plate, and then forced a servant who played on the bag-pipes, to pipe before them to the ship, whom they also detained, and was brought along with them to the *Marshalsea*, where he was sick till his release.

The next day they weighed anchor, and came to *Calf-Sound*, where the boatswain went ashore again with four armed men, meeting with no Plunder. From thence they went to the Island of *Eda*, to plunder the house of Mr. Fea, whom Gow had formerly been School-fellow with, and knowing him to be a Man of Courage, believed that the Alarm at *Caristoun* had drawn him thither: But Mr. Fea's wife at that time being very sick in bed, kept him at home, and having notice of them he sent a letter to Gow by James Laing, to desire him to withdraw, assuring him that most of the inhabitants were fled to the mountains on the report of his being a Pirate, desiring him to send the messenger safe back, at whose return the affrights of the people would be over. Gow sent him word back, that he would write to nobody, but if Mr. Fea would send his men with a Boat, he would reward them handsomely, which Mr. Fea hearing, he ordered his great Boat to be staved, and sunk, and the sails to be carried out of sight. In the mean time, perceiving Gow's boat come on shore, with five men in it, well armed, he met them, and said if they would go to a Publick House in the neighbourhood, and take a cup of ale with him, he would see what he could do to serve them, which they agreed to, seeing Mr. Fea was all alone, not suspecting any danger. Mr. Fea had before given orders for half a dozen men, well armed, to lie in ambush to surprize them, which being done, Mr. Fea sent to Mr. Gow to let him know, that the country was alarmed, and that it would be his best way peaceable to surrender, which Gow did in a day or two, thinking thereby to make himself an evidence; but it would not do, although he complied so far as to delude all his men ashore one after another, who would certainly have cut his throat, had they known of any ways afterwards to have escaped.

They were put on board the *Greyhound*, which delivered them into the *Marshalsea*, *March* 30, 1714, where they continued till June following, when eight of them were hanged at *Execution Dock*, viz. *John Gow, James Williams, James Belvin, John Winter, Peter Rawlisson, Daniel Mc.Cawley, William Ingram*, for another Piracy under *Anstis*, and a month afterwards *Alexander Rob* was hanged for Piracy under *Gow*.